A Brief History of
Christianity

Blackwell Brief Histories of
Religion

This series offers brief, accessible, and lively accounts of key topics within theology and religion. Each volume presents both academic and general readers with a selected history of topics which have had a profound effect on religious and cultural life. The word "history" is, therefore, understood in its broadest cultural and social sense. The volumes are based on serious scholarship but they are written engagingly and in terms readily understood by general readers.

Published

Alister E. McGrath – A Brief History of Heaven
G. R. Evans – A Brief History of Heresy
Tamara Sonn – A Brief History of Islam
Douglas J. Davies – A Brief History of Death
Lawrence S. Cunningham – A Brief History of Saints
Carter Lindberg – A Brief History of Christianity

A Brief History of
Christianity

CARTER LINDBERG

Blackwell
Publishing

Clinton College Library

© 2006 by Carter Lindberg

BLACKWELL PUBLISHING
350 Main Street, Malden, MA 02148-5020, USA
9600 Garsington Road, Oxford OX4 2DQ, UK
550 Swanston Street, Carlton, Victoria 3053, Australia

The right of Carter Lindberg to be identified as the Author of this
Work has been asserted in accordance with the UK Copyright,
Designs, and Patents Act 1988.

All rights reserved. No part of this publication may be
reproduced, stored in a retrieval system, or transmitted,
in any form or by any means, electronic, mechanical,
photocopying, recording or otherwise, except as permitted by
the UK Copyright, Designs, and Patents Act 1988, without the
prior permission of the publisher.

First published 2006 by Blackwell Publishing Ltd

2 2008

Library of Congress Cataloging-in-Publication Data

Lindberg, Carter, 1937–
    A brief history of Christianity / Carter Lindberg.
        p. cm. — (Blackwell brief histories of religion)
    Includes bibliographical references and index.
    ISBN 978-1-4051-1078-5 (hardcover: alk. paper)
    ISBN 978-1-4051-1047-1 (pbk.: alk. paper)
    1. Church history. I. Title. II. Series.

    BR145.3.L56 2005
    270—dc22
                                        2005006598

A catalogue record for this title is available from the British Library.

Set in 10/12.5pt Meridien
by Graphicraft Limited, Hong Kong
Printed and bound in Singapore
by Fabulous Printers Pte Ltd

The publisher's policy is to use permanent paper from mills that operate a
sustainable forestry policy, and which has been manufactured from pulp
processed using acid-free and elementary chlorine-free practices. Furthermore,
the publisher ensures that the text paper and cover board used have met
acceptable environmental accreditation standards.

For further information on
Blackwell Publishing, visit our website:
www.blackwellpublishing.com

To Teddy and Coco

Contents

Preface

A "brief" history of Christianity falls into the genre of the pro-verbial final exam question: provide a history of the universe with a couple of examples. While I hope the following effort will provide a bit more perspective on the history of Western Christianity than a variation on the theme of curious George goes to church, I am all too aware of what is missing in the following narrative. The task has proven to be more daunting than I had at first thought – though probably not as daunting as the proposed "brief history of eternity" we bandied about in discussing this proposal. After having taught a survey course on the history of Christianity for more years than I care to remember, I naively assumed I could just paste together all my old yellowed notes and that would be it. But even as cryptic as they were, far more cutting was required – even with the gracious allowance by the editors of more space. A very partial remedy for the topics suffering neglect is the list of suggested reading. The list is not a bibliography of works consulted, though some of course were, but resources for addressing the many omissions in the text. I have also attempted to avoid footnotes. Partially this decision was to save space, but it also reflects that fact that over the years

I have appropriated the insights of so many scholars that I no longer am aware of specific attributions. Peter of Blois (d. 1212) is justly renowned for his comment: "We are like dwarfs standing on the shoulders of giants; thanks to them, we see farther than they. Busying ourselves with the treatises written by the ancients, we take their choice thoughts." I haven't seen nearly as far as the giant scholars of the history of Christianity, but I am grateful for their broad shoulders for whatever panorama the following text provides, and I beg their forgiveness for not crediting them for their "choice thoughts."

I am also grateful to the editors of Blackwell Publishing, especially Rebecca Harkin, who has supported, but should not be blamed, for this effort; and Andrew Humphries, who not only saw this project into print but also chose excellent reviewers of the manuscript whose insightful criticisms and suggestions have vastly improved the text. In retrospect, I am also grateful now (I wasn't at the time!) to those colleagues of the School of Theology at Boston University who many years ago forced me to accept teaching the survey course. It turned out to be really great fun – mainly because of the generations of lively students who wouldn't allow it to be just a litany of dates. Finally, I am delighted to dedicate this volume to our most recent grandchildren – Theodore (Teddy) and Claudia (aka Coco) – who, like their cousins, provide great reasons to get out of the study and play.

Chapter 1

The Responsibility to Remember: An Introduction to the Historiography of Christianity

In a memorable epigram, the historian Richard Hofstadter stated: "Memory is the thread of personal identity, history of public identity." Memory and historical identity are inseparable. Most of us have experienced the embarrassment of momentarily forgetting a name in the midst of an introduction. Think what life would be like without any memory at all. Life is terribly difficult for an amnesiac, and it is tragic for the person – and his or her family and friends – with Alzheimer's disease. The loss of memory is not just the absence of "facts"; it is the loss of personal identity, family, friends, indeed the whole complex of life's meaning. It is very difficult if not impossible to function in society if we do not know who we are. Our memory is the thread of our personal identity.

What about our religious identities? Are we amnesiacs when someone asks how the Methodist or the Roman Catholic Church came to be? Beyond referring to our parents or a move to a new neighborhood, could we explain why we belong to St. Mary's by the gas station or the Lutheran church by the grocery store?

A French friend once began to explain contemporary French–German relations to me by referring to the significance of the ninth-century division of Charlemagne's empire! Most of us do not go back that far to understand the present, but his perspective illustrates the tenacity of historical memory, all too painfully evident in the eruption of historical ethnic conflicts. On the other hand, if we do not know our personal and communal histories, we are like children easily manipulated by those who would revise the past for their own purposes. Historical perspective is important for counteracting the tyranny of current opinions.

The biblical community has always known that its identity is rooted in history. Isaiah calls Israel to "Look to the rock from which you were hewn, and to the quarry from which your were dug. Look to Abraham your father and to Sarah who bore you" (Isaiah 51:1–2). The genealogies scattered through the Bible remind the people of God of their roots in creation and their destiny in God's plan (Matthew 1:1–25). Christian identity is clearly stated in the historical shorthand of the Christian creeds that confess faith in the historical person of Jesus who was born, suffered, and died. Christians put a unique spin on this history when they confess that this historical Jesus is also the historic Christ who was raised from the dead and who will return to complete history. Thus, from an insider's perspective, the identity of the Christian community is formed by both the historical past and the historical future. In brief, then, Christian identity is rooted in history, not in nature, philosophy, or ethics.

Sociologists suggest that our family identity is passed on to us through our conversations with the mothers and fathers who have gone on before us. We know, of course, from even limited family experience that when we no longer talk to our parents and children we begin to forget who we are. This is not to say that conversations between generations are always pleasant, but to say that they are important for learning "how we got this way." To paraphrase the old saw about watching the making of sausage and political decisions, the study of our personal and communal histories, including the history of Christianity, may be disturbing. But without such conversations we are condemned to presentism, which is a more elegant way of describing a continuous "me generation."

Historical memory provides perspective, a horizon, for judging what is or is not important. Without a horizon it is too easy to overvalue what is before your nose. A horizon enables the valuation of the relative significance of everything within this horizon, as near or far, great or small. The idea of horizon or historical distance bears further reflection.

Historical distance can be a surprising element for understanding the present. Fernand Braudel, the renowned French historian, spoke of this by analogy to living in a foreign city. If you live in a foreign city for a year you may not learn a great deal about that city, but when you return home you will be surprised by your increasing comprehension as well as questions of your homeland. You did not previously understand or perhaps even perceive these characteristics because you were too close to them. Likewise, a visit to the past provides distance and a vantage point for comprehending and questioning the present. In other words, distance – in history as in navigation – is necessary for finding true bearings. Sailors, at least those with some longevity, do not navigate by watching the prow of the boat. Hence the old adage about people who can't see beyond their own noses applies equally to historical myopia.

I have belabored the importance of memory and history for our personal and communal identities because we live in a culture that regards as wisdom Henry Ford's dictum that "history is bunk." I hope the image of the amnesiac will jar loose easy acquiescence to forgetfulness of the past and warn us of the dangers posed by lack of identity. Without a sense of our communal and personal history we are prey for whatever fads and fancies appeal to us. If we do not recognize the role of history in shaping our identities then we unreflectively allow the past to control us. This may not have bad results but it puts us in the position of being misled by those who wish to manipulate us.

Tradition and Confession

Lack of historical consciousness promotes a conversational deficit in the communion of saints, the church. The irony is that this is occurring even as we are acquiring more and more information. We now have a wealth of archeological and textual materials, including texts from the early Christian community not included in the Bible, far beyond the wildest imagination of medieval scribes, but without an interpretive tradition it is difficult to know what to do with this wealth of material.

"Tradition" is not merely a mass of information, but in its root sense means the action of handing on an understanding of that information, not just its rote repetition. The prolific historian of doctrine Jaroslav Pelikan sharpens this point with his clever distinction between tradition and traditionalism: "Tradition is the living faith of the dead; traditionalism is the dead faith of the living." In the Bible and the church fathers, "tradition" means primarily God's self-revelation; God's handing himself over in Jesus. Thus the fundamental structure of the Christian faith and community depends upon tradition, upon passing on significant conversations with prior generations concerning God's activity in history.

In the New Testament, Paul speaks of handing on what he has received. The first place he speaks this way is in connection with the Eucharist (1 Corinthians 11:23–26); the second place is where he cites the confession of the cross and resurrection of Jesus (1 Corinthians 15:3–11). The concept of the tradition as the passing on of the news that God has handed over his Son at a particular moment in world history for the salvation of humankind is bound up in the New Testament with the concept of remembering (Greek: *anamnesis*, i.e., the exact opposite of forgetting, amnesia). It is no accident that these terms are both present in connection with the Eucharist or Lord's Supper. The tradition that Paul cites presents an exhortation to *anamnesis*. The meal that Jesus held with his disciples the night before his death will continue to be held "in remembrance of me." This is not just a conceptual remembrance, an idea; rather, it is a carrying out of the remembrance that offers, passes on, his presence itself. This "doing in remembrance" has its model in the Hebrew Bible, namely in the Passover as the remembrance of the flight from Egypt. Here too the past event is made present as every co-celebrant becomes a contemporary of the event through remembrance of what is passed on. The essential yet paradoxical point in the biblical understanding of tradition is that it is not fixed upon the past, but that in presenting the past (i.e., making the past present) it has significance for a new future.

Chapter 2

The Law of Praying is
the Law of Believing

The title of this chapter is from Prosper of Aquitaine (ca. 390–
ca. 463): "The rule of prayer should lay down the rule of faith." By
his time, the Christian community had developed from the small
group of Jewish followers of Jesus worshipping in the temple in
Jerusalem (Acts 2:46), to the established religion of the Roman
Empire with scriptures, creeds, and a hierarchical authority all
claiming to be "apostolic." This astounding development was
marked by tumult and controversy within and without as the
various Christian communities with all the pluralism of their
theologies and writings created a self-identity that would in turn
inform and identify Western culture up to our own time. In the
process, the "rule of faith" was not determined by "prayer alone"
but with the help of tough, hard-nosed, and bright leaders who
vigorously opposed alternative Christian writings, theologies, and
ways of life as well as challenges from rival religious perspectives.
The Christian protagonists and antagonists in these developments
believed salvation depended on to whom one prayed, that is,
what one believed and confessed about God and salvation. Normative authorities were needed to answer Jesus' question: "But
who do you say that I am?" (Matthew 16:15).

In retrospect, the Christian community believed that its survival was the fulfillment of God's plan. "Now after John was arrested, Jesus came to Galilee, proclaiming the good news of God, and saying, 'The time is fulfilled, and the kingdom of God has come near; repent, and believe in the good news'" (Mark 1:14–15).

"The time is fulfilled." The author of Mark wrote in Greek, and as the saying goes, the Greeks have a word for it. The Greek word used in the above sentence is "kairos," that is, the time for a decision, the time when events are so juxtaposed that a crucial decision or event may occur. Another Greek word for time is "chronos," that is, "chronological" time measured by units of years, days, hours, minutes, etc. "Kairos" has the potential to qualitatively change "chronos." The early Christian community had this sense that the appearance of Jesus in the midst of chronological time marked a crucial (crux, "cross") moment, a time of decision. A "kairotic" event divides time in terms of what precedes and succeeds it. This is what early Christian historians were getting at when they proclaimed Jesus the Christ is the center of history between the creation and the Last Judgment; a conviction eventually enshrined in the dating by years before and after Christ (BC and AD) or in more recent terms before and during the common era of Judaism and Christianity (BCE and CE). The "kairos" occurred at the "chronos" of a number of developments: the dispersion of Judaism, the dominance of the Roman Empire, and the universality of Hellenistic culture.

The early Christian community was convinced the "time is fulfilled" because they believed Jesus was the fulfillment of God's promise to Israel. Persuaded by their experience of Easter that Jesus is the Messiah, the early Christians – themselves Jews – therefore saw the promises in the Hebrew Bible to be transferable to Jesus. Convinced that God gave "all authority in heaven and earth" to Jesus, his followers believed they had the mission to "make disciples of all nations, baptizing them in the name of the Father and of the Son and of the Holy Spirit" (Matthew 28:18–19).

The early community's liturgical confessions and hymns testify to its conviction that Jesus fulfilled the promise God made through his prophets (Romans 1:1–4). In this perspective, history is viewed within the context of God's plan of salvation "that was kept secret for long ages but is now disclosed, and through the prophetic writings is made known" (Romans 16:25–26). Rooted in the life, preaching, and death of Jesus of Nazareth, the early Christian community initially saw itself as a renewal movement within Palestinian Judaism; Easter confirmed God's promises to Israel.

The historical context for Christianity thus first of all is the whole history of Israel and its sacred scriptures, the Bible of early Christianity (there is not an "Old" Testament until the church developed the "New" Testament some 200 years later). As initially a Jewish movement, Christianity was heir to the plurality of influences from the Hebrew Bible, diaspora Judaism, and Hellenistic Judaism. Furthermore, in its formative stages, Christianity benefited from the protective shield Judaism provided as a "licit" religion in the Roman Empire.

At the time of the early Christian community, Jews had long been widely dispersed in Asia Minor and the Roman Empire with sizeable populations in urban centers such as Rome and Alexandria. The Jewish Dispersion (Diaspora), with its origins in the Assyrian and Babylonian deportations beginning in the eighth century BCE, provided a point of contact for Christian missionaries who "proclaimed the word of God in the synagogues of the Jews" (Acts 13:5), addressing both Jews and their Gentile converts (Acts 13:42–43; 14:1; 17:1–4; 17:10–17). The Book of Acts repeatedly states that in his missionary travels Paul would go to the local synagogue "every Sabbath" where he would argue and "try to convince Jews and Greeks" (Acts 18:4).

The ethical monotheism of Judaism appealed to those "Greeks," that is Gentiles, of the Greco-Roman Empire who found philosophical ethics too cerebral and Dionysian religions too emotional and amoral. The drawback however was that Gentile conversion to Judaism included male circumcision and obedience to ritual and dietary laws. The appeal of Christianity was an ethical monotheism without such restrictive and counter-cultural rules. In Christ "neither circumcision nor uncircumcision counts for anything; the only thing that counts is faith working through love" (Galatians 5:6). Furthermore, Christianity appealed to the marginalized, women and the poor, in the proclamation of social equality. "There is no longer Jew or Greek, there is no longer slave or free, there is no longer male and female, for all of you are one in Christ Jesus" (Galatians 3:28).

In a society that blamed the victim, the biblical motif of the great reversal – that the last shall be first and the first last – pointedly expressed in the "Magnificat" (Luke 1:46–55) must have appealed to those on the receiving end of the Roman view that the gods rewarded the good with wealth and punished the evil and lazy with poverty. That God would side with the poor and oppressed was a discordant note to those whose worldview was shaped by the Roman poet Ovid's (43 BCE–CE 17) dictum, "property confers rank," but it was a message of hope to the disenfranchised.

It has been said that the blood of the martyrs is the seed of the church. "Martyr" derives from the Greek word for witness, and in that sense the witness of the early Christians that won Gentiles to the church was not only the witness in the face of persecution, but also the witness of serving the neighbor (cf. Matthew 25:35–40). There are numerous references from the early church fathers concerning the collection of funds during worship that are dedicated to helping the needy. One of the more famous stories is that of Laurence (d. 258), a deacon of Rome who was told by the civil authorities to deliver up the treasure of the church. In response he assembled the poor to whom he had distributed the church's possessions and presented them to the Roman prefect with the words, "These are the treasure of the church." The prefect was not amused, and – the story goes – had Laurence slowly roasted to death on a gridiron. Tertullian (ca. 160–ca. 225) summarized the point when he stated to Roman culture, "our compassion spends more in the street than yours does in the temples."

The Roman Empire and its Political Achievements

The early Christian conviction that Jesus is the Messiah, whom God sent in the fullness of time, meant to them that universal history was prepared for this event. The Roman Empire was thus part of God's providential plan. The *pax romana* had pacified the Mediterranean world and suppressed robbery and piracy along the Roman roads and seaways. The network of roads enabled shipping, commerce and communications – from the British Isles to North Africa, from the Iberian Peninsula to the Near East – and thus facilitated the spread of Christian missions. Roman law also enabled missionary mobility. Paul could travel with relative safety and could appeal to his Roman citizenship when in difficulty (Acts 25:1–12).

Hellenization and its Cultural Achievements

The Greek language of the time, "Koine," was the common language of diplomacy and commerce in the Mediterranean world. Practically everyone understood Koine. Indeed, the culture, especially in the cities and commercial centers, was multilingual. Linguistic universality enabled Christians to spread their message rapidly. Thus early Christian missionaries not only did not have to spend years in language school before setting out to spread their faith, but with their facility with the "lingua franca" of their day they did not appear as an ethnic minority. Furthermore, their scripture (i.e., the Hebrew Bible) was already in a Greek translation known as the "Septuagint" or "LXX" (after the supposed number of translators in the legendary account of its origin). By around 100 BCE the bulk of the Old Testament was circulating in Greek.

Hellenism also created a universal cultural orientation that was not only esteemed and perpetuated by the Romans but was also present in Palestine and influential upon Judaism. Spread by the conquests of Alexander the Great (356–323 BCE), Hellenistic culture provided a common philosophical terminology. Christians borrowed freely from both the terminology of Greek philosophy and its claim to be ancient wisdom. With regard to the latter claim, as we note in the appendix, the early Christians agreed that older is better. Thus, to counter the charge of innovation, defenders of the Christian faith claimed that Christianity goes back to Moses who is even before the ancient philosophers so highly esteemed in the Hellenistic culture of the day. A classic example of the use of philosophical terminology is the Christian use of the term and concept "logos." The term was rich with philosophical meanings as the universal "reason" or "word" that governs and permeates the world. The prologue to the Fourth Gospel gives this a new twist when it proclaims that the logos is not merely an idea but God incarnate: "In the beginning was the Word ["logos"] . . . And the Word became flesh and lived among us" (John 1:1–14). The claim that Christianity is really *the* true philosophy served as a catchy entrée to missionary dialogue, but would in turn be attacked by other Christians as warping the gospel message.

In fact control of the gospel message became an increasing priority as Christian communities developed throughout the empire, often with their own local take on Jesus supported by their own teachers and writings claiming to go back to particular apostles or their disciples. Without an authoritative scripture, how could one know the right teaching (literally, "orthodoxy"), but without the right teaching, how could one know which of the many scriptures extant among the various Christian communities were authoritative? These symbiotic problems stimulated the creation of an authoritative list of New Testament writings even while the early church was dealing with a number of other interrelated concerns at the same time.

Development of the Biblical Canon

Christianity, like Judaism and later Islam, is a religion of the book. It would be difficult to overestimate the significance of the determination of normative biblical writings for the history of the church and its faith. Indeed, the development of the canon of scriptures was the first dogmatic development in the history of Christianity; it has remained fundamental for most Christian communities down to today as *the* source for the Christian faith.

The word "canon" (Greek: *kanon*, "measuring rod") means "rule" or "standard." The Greek and Latin fathers applied the term canon beyond the list of scriptures, for example to lists of church rules, thus canon law; lists of saints or heroes of the faith, thus persons who are canonized. The death of the first Christian generation and the efforts by various Christian communities or individuals to introduce their alternative understandings of Jesus and salvation led to the development of the canon. Since salvation related to confessing Christ, it was crucial to have the right confession and thus the right scripture by which to "measure" that confession. A famous (or infamous as the case may be) example, often cited as a major impetus to the formation of the New Testament, is the canon of Marcion (ca. 100–ca.160). Reputedly the excommunicated son of the bishop of Sinope, a city on the southern shore of the Black Sea, Marcion became very wealthy in the shipping industry. Around 140, he moved to Rome, joined the church there, and made a huge benevolence gift for the mission of the church.

Marcion's theology presented a dualistic opposition between the world of the spirit (deemed good) and the world of matter (deemed evil). In brief, what concerned Marcion was his perceived opposition between the righteousness of the law as he understood it in the Hebrew Bible and the righteousness of faith in the New Testament. To Marcion, the Jewish God of law and wrath and the Christian God of love and mercy were mutually exclusive. Jesus the Christ was not truly a part of the material world created by the God of the Old Testament, but rather only appeared to be human, "in the likeness of sinful flesh" (Romans 8:3), in order to reveal the supreme God of love and fool the Old Testament God. Therefore, Marcion argued, the God of the Old Testament must be rejected in favor of the God of the New Testament, who in the person of Jesus saves people from the God of the Jews. To support his views, Marcion set forth a canon of scripture that completely excluded the Old Testament and included only the epistles of Paul (omitting 1 and 2 Timothy and Titus) expurgated of "Jewish" influences and a form of the Gospel of Luke, perhaps because he accepted the claim that the author was a companion of Paul. Paul, according to Marcion, was the only apostle who rightly understood that Christians are no longer under the law; the Judaistic errors of the other apostles blinded them to the truth.

The Roman church rejected Marcion's views and his canon, excommunicated him, and returned his large donation. Undeterred, Marcion went on to establish numerous Marcionite churches throughout Asia Minor, attestations to the attractiveness of his views. Further testimony to his success in mission were his many significant opponents, including Irenaeus of Lyons (ca. 130–ca. 200), Tertullian (ca. 160–ca. 225), and Justin Martyr (ca. 100–ca. 165), and not least the stimulus to speed up the process of fixing the authoritative list of writings that would become the New Testament. The decision to include the Old Testament was a doctrinal decision of great significance for the church's affirmation of its Jewish roots, and its understanding of creation, redemption, and Christian life in the world. Furthermore, the fixing of the New Testament canon also clearly affirms that valid and binding knowledge of God's revelation in Jesus Christ may be gained only from these writings. Other writings have certainly been and continue to be significant for the faith and life of the church, but they cannot claim the same authority in the church as the canonical scriptures.

As already noted, the process of fixing the New Testament canon was a circular one in which the gospel message was used to determine the writings that were to be the "canonical" source – the measuring rod – of the gospel message. Although the earliest writings of Paul date from about 50 CE, it was not until the latter half of the second century that challenges such as Marcion and prophetic movements such as Montanism that claimed revelations inspired by the Holy Spirit impelled the church to determine its canon. How did the early church decide which Christian writings should be included in the canon? The answer to this question involves a complex and long historical process that we can only generalize about here.

One of the criteria is that indicated by our opening reference to Prosper of Aquitaine: a writing's normative use in worship. Thus, Justin Martyr, who died in Rome about 165, reported about written "memories" of the apostles and their disciples that contained the words of Jesus, called Gospels, that were read during Sunday worship. A second criterion is that a "canonical" writing had to reflect tradition thought to be apostolic in origin. And a third criterion is that the writing be "catholic," that is, universal in the sense of enjoying widespread use in the churches. The process of canonization had a strong community orientation. Here we see the interrelationship of community and canonicity so succinctly expressed by Augustine (354–430): "I would not believe the gospel unless the Catholic Church moved me." In brief, the Bible is the church's book developed in the worshipping community, the community that professes and confesses Jesus is Lord.

It appears that most of the 27 books now constituting the New Testament were in common usage in the church by the end of the second century. The earliest extant list of New Testament books is the Muratorian fragment, named for the Italian scholar Ludovico Muratori who discovered it in a library in Milan and published it in 1740. Held to date from the late second century, the fragment includes the four Gospels, Acts, all 13 Pauline epistles, and rejects the Marcionite epistles of Paul to Laodicea and Alexandria as forgeries. The list also includes Jude, 1 and 2 John, the Wisdom of Solomon, the Apocalypse of John, and the Apocalypse of Peter, with the caveat that the latter is not accepted everywhere. It also mentions the Shepherd of Hermas as an edifying book but that it is too recent to be included in the canon. It does not include 1 and 2 Peter, James, and one Johannine epistle. The oldest witness to the complete New Testament as it now stands is Athanasius (ca. 296–373), the bishop of Alexandria. In 367, in his annual pastoral letter to the churches of Egypt that set that year's date for Easter, he listed the books to be accepted as canonical literature: the four Gospels, Acts, 14 letters of Paul including Hebrews, 7 catholic epistles, and Revelation. The Greek church accepted this list, as did also the Synod of Rome (382) under Pope Damasus I. Athanasius' list was promoted by Augustine and accepted at the North African synods of Hippo (393) and Carthage (397). Thus, by the beginning of the fifth century, there was a common agreement on the canon of the New Testament in most of the churches. Somewhat of an exception was the Syrian church that up to the fifth century had a shorter canon and used the Diatessaron, a synoptic harmony of the four Gospels composed around 170 by Tatian, a Syrian church father.

The Christian community by the fourth and fifth centuries was now handing on the gospel message not only in oral form but also in written form. Already by the end of the second century, Irenaeus, the bishop of Lyons, insisted that the rule of faith is faithfully preserved by the church and finds multiform expression in the canonical books. The gospel preached in the churches continues in scripture. We could speak of an "inscripturization" of the apostolic proclamation that is the foundation of the faith. Thus, for Irenaeus, the Christian community does not "create" the canon, but acknowledges it. The church receives and conserves the rule of faith. From the perspective of the church, this is not something secret or mysterious but a public transmission – handing on (*traditio*) – of the gospel under the guidance of the Holy Spirit who permeates the church.

As Tertullian maintained, only the person who belongs to the true, orthodox church is authorized for the exposition of scripture. And the only true support for an orthodox interpretation of scripture over against the variations of individual interpretations is the rule of faith. The rule of faith, the shorthand for the later Trinitarian creeds, structured the responses of catechumens at their baptism to the questions, "Do you believe in God the Father Almighty?" "Do you believe in Jesus Christ his only Son our Lord?" "Do you believe in the Holy Spirit?" There is here the reciprocal relationship between the New Testament canon and the community's confession of faith. Scripture, therefore, according to 2 Peter 1:20, is not a "matter of one's own interpretation."

The canon determined the identity of holy scripture. While the fixing of the canon was a foundational decision by the church, and thereby the source for future theological reflection, it did not guarantee the unity of the church. It became apparent that even such a small collection of writings could yield alternative answers to Jesus' question, "Who do you say that I am?" In response, the church continued to spell out its faith in the form of creeds.

Chapter 3

Sibling Rivalry:
Heresy, Orthodoxy, and
Ecumenical Councils

The early Christian community understood itself in continuity with Israel, God's chosen people. Yet Christians prayed to the risen Jesus, their Lord – a blasphemous act to their fellow Jews because it went counter to exclusive devotion to God: "Hear, O Israel: The Lord is our God, the Lord alone" (Deuteronomy 6:4). The first sibling rivalry then was between the Jews who confessed Jesus is the Messiah and those who rejected this claim as blasphemous. Again we see the locus of tension in worship – the law of praying is the law of believing. As the Christian community was forced from the temple and began its mission to the Gentiles, further rivalries arose as the Christian communities first rejected Greco-Roman culture and then began to appropriate it. The developing church thus strove to delineate its faith in Jesus in relation to both its Jewish roots and heritage on the one hand and the Hellenistic context into which it was moving on the other hand. This is the context for the development of formal confessions of faith: creeds. Those who chose and advocated confessions that conflicted with what the church believed, taught, and confessed came to be called heretics (from the Greek, *hairesis*, "a choosing"). The issues about which the confessions developed focused on the relationship of Jesus to God and the relationship of Jesus to humankind; the Christian claim in both issues is that in Jesus one definitively encounters God's own self.

The Structure of Tradition: Confession and Doctrine

The passing on of the tradition concerning Jesus the Christ occurred from the very beginning of the Christian community in many different ways, among others in the form of confessions of faith for catechumens preparing for baptism (1 Corinthians 15:3–6) and the command to proclaim the gospel (Matthew 28:19). Such confessions formulated central statements of the faith and very early became expressions of ecclesial consensus, traditionally termed "orthodoxy." These confessions had to an increasing extent the function of validating ecclesial teaching, and as a "rule of faith" that defined apostolic teaching they governed the proclamation of the gospel and served to detect heterodoxy and heresy. Such validating teaching in the churches, together with the developing canon of apostolic writings and the churches' office of bishop, functioned to preserve the identity of the church in conformity to the gospel. At this point it can only be noted that considerable problems have arisen in the history of Christianity in relation to the relationship between apostolic writings (the Bible), the apostolic creeds, and the apostolic office of bishop.

The form of confessions reflected the language, concepts, and culture of the particular times of their formulations, as well as the questions and issues uppermost in the mind of the community at the time. This was not a tidy process; what one community or generation believed "orthodox" could appear to the next as problematic or even heretical. What the church believes, teaches, and confesses is therefore not a collection of timeless truths but the historical expression of the community's convictions. Thus confessions such as the classic creeds (Apostles',

Nicene, and Athanasian), as well as later confessions such as in the Reformation period and the Barmen Declaration against Nazism, are provisional expressions that both express and form Christian identities in history.

Doctrine as a Key to Christian Memory and Identity

It is a popular modern cliché that religion should be free of doctrine. This reflects both the awareness that doctrine has been a source of intolerance and that doctrine is historically conditioned. The modern development of historical relativism that posits doctrines are historically contingent has also eroded their role in the maintenance of Christian memory. The very phrase "history of doctrine" denotes the modern dilemma of trying to mesh what appear to be antithetical phenomena. "History" denotes relativity and change, whereas "doctrine" connotes unchanging truths.

However, the Christian community has for most of its history held that without a grasp of and commitment to what the church has believed, taught, and confessed over the centuries, the church will be prey to what we may call "chameleonism," that is, it will take on the coloring of its environment. And reflecting the environment means losing or suppressing the church's memory and identity. As the saying goes, salt without savor should be thrown out.

The acknowledgment of doctrines in imperial law contributed to their character as infallible propositions. This is also how doctrine acquired the overtones of compulsion, as those who did not subscribe to the dogmatic decisions of the church were banished or worse by the state. But doctrine need not be conceived this way. To use a homely analogy: doctrine has too often been perceived as an electric fence designed to keep the ecclesiastical cows from straying far from home. If such an ecclesial cow is foolish enough to stray, she will be zapped. In the temporal realm, until recently, the electrical current was supplied by the state. Now, with the separation of church and state, the power is turned off; and with the rise of historical relativism, the fences themselves are largely gone. Therefore it may be more helpful to return to an earlier understanding of doctrine as analogous to a feed box, the purpose of which is to gather the herd by providing nourishment. This image correlates well with our earlier comments that link tradition with the Lord's Supper. Confession and its articulation in doctrine serve to nourish the self-understanding and identity of the Christian community. For the early church the purpose of dogma was both to develop the community's reflection on salvation wrought by God through Jesus and to impart meaning to earlier reflections that was not originally perceived.

There has never been a time when Christians did not face the task of expressing their faith in the form of confessions (a kind of shorthand of the faith). From the outset, the community was called to answer Jesus' question: "But who do you say that I am?" (Matthew 16:15), and to defend the hope Jesus inspired (1 Peter 3:15). The community's self-definition also needed to be maintained in the face of internal and external challenges. At their best, these endeavors were not ecclesiastical power trips or intellectual parlor games, but served as norms for worship and proclamation of the gospel. In other words, doctrine makes no sense outside the worshipping community. Doctrine was not intended to explain the mystery of God, but confess it. Doctrines are the consequence of baptism, Eucharist, preaching, evangelism, mission, and opposition to and dialogue with rival religions; doctrines arose from the liturgy (literally, "the work of the people"), from worship. That is why the Nicene and Apostles' creeds are often embedded in worship services.

Certainly, it has sometimes been the case that confessions and doctrines have been used to externalize and formalize the faith. Nevertheless, without doctrine, without confession, the church was in danger of no longer knowing what it believed. What the church believes, teaches, and confesses is the community's affirmation that "not anything goes."

Heresy

Orthodoxy is the language that preserves the promise character of the gospel, that salvation is received from God, not achieved by humans. In contrast, heresy is the language that in one or another way vitiates the promise of the gospel by making it contingent upon human achievement. It is important to realize at the outset that the historical relationship of heresy and orthodoxy is complex. The early church did not begin with a handy catalogue of orthodox dogmas by which to determine the presence of heresies. Rather, heresy and orthodoxy grew together in mutual interaction. That historical process was so complex that it will be useful to begin with a formal way to conceive of heresy; to get a sense of what the Christian community believed to be at stake as they developed their confessions of faith. Friedrich Schleiermacher (1768–1834), one of the most influential theologians of the nineteenth century, provided just such a useful formal way to conceive of heresy. "Now, if the distinctive essence of Christianity consists in the fact that in it all religious emotions are related to the redemption wrought by Jesus of Nazareth, there will be two ways in which heresy can arise . . . *Either* human nature will be so defined that a redemption in the strict sense cannot be accomplished, *or* the Redeemer will be defined in such a way that He cannot accomplish redemption."

Schleiermacher continues by positing that each option has two basic forms. Anthropological heresies (i.e., those defining human nature in ways that preclude redemption) either conceive of human nature as so intrinsically good that redemption is not necessary or as so intrinsically evil that redemption is impossible. The classical expressions of these positions are associated with Pelagianism (the former) and Manichaeism (the latter). Soteriological (from Greek *soter*, "savior") heresies (i.e., those defining the Redeemer in ways that preclude redemption) either conceive of the nature of Jesus as so like that of humankind that he lacks the power to redeem or as so different from that of humankind that there is no point of contact. The classical expressions of these positions are Ebionitism (the former) and Docetism (the latter). Logically, how one conceives of theological anthropology influences the conception of soteriology and vice versa; that is, these heresies are bound in pairs. Thus a Pelagian view of humankind as basically good will tend to view Jesus in Ebionite terms as a human being whose contribution is little more than moral instruction or guidance in the way of salvation. Historically, this has been the orientation of rationalism. The problem of humankind is perceived as ignorance of the good, and Jesus is the teacher and model of the good life. A Manichaean view that humankind is so evil that no God worth his salt would participate in human life will view Jesus in Docetic terms (i.e., as only an apparent person). Historically, this has been the orientation of supernaturalism or strict dualism.

Schleiermacher's formal definition of heresy is useful but not foolproof in efforts to unravel the historically tangled skein of heresy and orthodoxy. Hence, Schleiermacher cautioned "it is highly important that people should go to work with the greatest caution when it comes to declaring anything heretical." Such caution, however, appeared to be in short supply in the bitter disputes that racked the early church. Since we are engaged in a *brief* history, we shall focus on the central dogmatic developments: the doctrines of the Trinity and Christology.

Jesus' Relationship to God: The Doctrine of the Trinity

The fundamental doctrines of the Trinity and Christology have to do, respectively, with Jesus' relationship with God and with humankind. While the doctrine of the Trinity is associated with the Councils of Nicaea (325) and Constantinople (381), and the doctrine of Christology with the Council of Chalcedon (451), it is important to realize once again that historical developments are not very tidy, and that both doctrines developed simultaneously.

The historical context of the development of the doctrine of the Trinity was framed not only by theological disputes among and within the urban centers of Christianity but also very significantly by the rise of the "imperial church." By the early fourth century the sporadic imperial persecutions of Christians ceased and leading thinkers in the church were carrying on constructive dialogues with Greco-Roman culture. In 312, Constantine, earlier proclaimed ruler of the western provinces by the Roman army in Britain, led his troops south into Italy and victoriously entered Rome after fierce battles against the larger army of the Roman emperor Maxentius. Prior to the final battle at the Milvian Bridge outside Rome, Constantine reportedly had a vision of the cross with the promise that under this sign he would conquer. He then replaced the emblems on the shields and standards of his troops with an intersecting X-P. Whether Constantine had in mind the emblem of the Sun god, Sol invictus, of whom he was then a devotee, or the first two letters of the Greek word for Christ (*chi* – "X," *rho* – "P") as Christian propagandists would later claim, the outcome was a change in policy toward the Christian faith. It was said that Constantine attributed his victory to the God of the Christians. In 324 he defeated his Eastern rival, Licinius, under the same standard and thus became sole master of the Greco-Roman world until his death in 337.

The Christian church now had an imperial patron. In 313 the Edict of Milan not only granted Christians freedom of worship but also restored church property taken during the persecutions, whether held by individuals or the state. Constantine's wife, Fausta, gave her palace on the Lateran to the church, and numerous other properties and monies soon followed. In 321 Constantine legalized bequests to the church, and its income was now also supplemented by the estates of all those who died without an heir; a firm foundation for the growing wealth of the church was established. The clergy were granted immunity from various civil responsibilities; bishops were provided imperial support for travel and administration; and the jurisdiction of church courts began extending to civil matters such as the manumission of slaves.

Constantine also displaced the many "immortal gods," hitherto seen as the protectors of the empire, with the God of Christianity. The French kings would later express this drive for a unified empire in their phrase: "one king, one law, one faith." In this regard sociologists of religion speak of the role religion plays in the construction of society by providing an ontological basis for civil institutions. That is, the society and its institutions are rooted in the mind of God. Almost immediately, however, Constantine discovered that the Christian faith he believed would be the glue to cement in place his vast empire was functioning in some major areas more as a corrosive acid eating away at the desired social unity.

The focal point for the spread of disunity in the church and hence the danger to the newly united empire was Alexandria. The size and cultural significance of Alexandria ranked it second only to Rome, and its renown as a center of Christian learning was already widespread in the second and third centuries in connection with the catechetical school led most famously by Clement (ca. 190–ca. 202) and then Origen (ca. 202–31). The theologian who created the crisis for the church and for Constantine was Arius (ca. 256–336), a priest in the port district of the city, popular among his parishioners for his preaching and ascetic life. The controversy associated with Arius concerned the relationship of Jesus to God. Arius emphasized the one God's absolute transcendence and indivisibility. Therefore, since God's substance cannot be shared with any other being – for then God would be divisible and changeable, a horror to Greek metaphysics – everything that exists outside of God – including Christ – must be created from nothing. Christ, the Word of God, did not exist prior to his creation by God; hence the famous phrase of the Arians: "there was [a time] when he [Christ] was not." Arius was concerned to maintain a Christian monotheism against what appeared to him to be the introduction of ideas of change in the Godhead. Ironically, his opponents thought that Arius ran the danger of presenting Christ as a demigod, and thus the question arose as to how this differed from pagan polytheism. Furthermore, it appeared that Arius was claiming that Christ's perfection was not therefore in his nature, his being one in substance with God, but in his voluntary fulfillment of God's will. In following or imitating Christ, therefore, humankind can also attain favor with God through ethical progress. This was a theology of salvation that appealed to the largest and most influential group of "spiritual athletes" of the day, the monks. Hence it was a brilliant propaganda coup when Arius' later opponent, Athanasius, wrote a *Life of Antony*, the most revered of the Egyptian ascetics, that argued that Antony's holiness was a gift of God's grace, not an ethical achievement.

Arius' views spread widely thanks to his persuasive rhetoric and ability to cast his theology in verse to popular tunes so that even the dockworkers of Alexandria began to propagate his theology. The consequent turmoil led his bishop, Alexander of Alexandria, to call upon him and his "Ariomaniacs" to recant. Arius refused, fled, and enlisted support from a number of bishops in northwestern Asia Minor. The controversy was not easily settled by appealing to scripture, for each side found biblical passages to support their position. Arius cited Colossians that Christ was "the firstborn of all creation" (Colossians 1:15), and his opponents appealed to the affirmation in the Gospel of John (1:1–5) that the "Word was with God . . . in the beginning."

As the controversy raged on, Constantine became increasingly concerned that religious division would erode political unity. After fruitless appeals for harmony, Constantine called a council of all the bishops to meet in Nicaea. This was not an invitation the bishops could refuse! All told, though there are no extant accurate lists of attendees, between 220 and 300 bishops assembled at Nicaea in 325. This was the first ecumenical council (Greek: *oikoumene*, "the inhabited world," i.e., universal, meaning in practical terms, the empire). The significance of this meeting would reverberate theologically and institutionally throughout the history of the church. Theologically, the council formulated a creed that rejected the Arian doctrine that Christ, the Son, was not of the same substance of God, the Father; and also rejected the Arian teaching that Christ is the Son by virtue of his will. The council affirmed that the Son is of the same substance (*homoousios*) of the Father.

Institutionally, Constantine's calling of the council presaged centuries of struggles between church and empire that would continue up to the last crowning of an emperor, that of Napoleon. From Constantine's perspective he had the right to call a council because in the context of Greco-Roman culture the emperor represented God on earth, and was thus legally entitled to intervene in religious affairs. The council itself was procedurally modeled on the Roman Senate. This allowed the bishops relative autonomy in resolving doctrinal issues because the emperor did not have the right to vote in the Senate. But Constantine did confirm the decisions of the bishops and made them binding under Roman law.

From the Council of Nicaea to the Council of Constantinople

In 328 Athanasius became the bishop of Alexandria. His genius was to formulate the rule: "All that is said of the Father is also said of the Son, except that the Son is Son, and not Father." But Athanasius did not become the "father of catholic orthodoxy" without a long and costly struggle. Immediately after Nicaea, Arius was condemned and exiled. Yet not all the council fathers were pleased by the use of the Nicene term *homoousios*, a term central to Athanasius' argument. Constantine allowed an anti-Nicene coalition to take root in his court and by the end of his reign it had become an anti-Athanasian force. As bishop, Athanasius was soon faced by riots and intrigues against the Nicene party. He stood firm, but by the time of Constantine's death and the succession of his sons, the leaders of the Nicene party in the East had been deposed or exiled. A relentless and dirty campaign began against Athanasius. Since his opponents could not attack his orthodoxy, they attacked his person, accusing him, among other things, of murdering another bishop and using his hand in magic rites – a charge refuted by producing the person in question with both hands still attached. In 335 Athanasius was banished to Trier. The attempt to rehabilitate Arius was prevented by his death in a public lavatory in 336 – a sign to the orthodox party of God's judgment.

On the eve of the Council of Constantinople (381), the Cappadocian bishop, Gregory of Nyssa (d. 394), declared that it was the destiny of his time to bring to full clarity the mystery that in the New Testament was only dimly intimated. A daring pronouncement, but it outlined the theological task of the day. The emperor Theodosius (379–95) sealed the peace with the imperial Council of Constantinople that endorsed the Council of Nicaea and also defined the divinity of the Holy Spirit. He also outlawed the Arians.

The Nicene-Constantinopolitan creed quickly became the baptismal creed of the East and also became popular in the West. It was incorporated in the eucharistic liturgy and used in East and West, and continues to be regarded as a truly ecumenical and therefore catholic summation of the Christian faith.

The development of the "Nicene" creed differs from the creation of the New Testament canon and the rule of faith in that its specific concern is the doctrine of God. By means of this doctrine the church erected a barrier against the Hellenism that threatened to inundate the Christian faith. Neither council attempted to plumb the depth of the divine mystery or to define God's essence.

Their intention was to indicate that God himself encounters us in Jesus Christ and that in the Holy Spirit God himself is present with the church. That the councils were not in their own self-understanding eliminating all theological reflection may be seen in the continuing reflection on these dogmas in the history of the church. One of the next persons to take up this task was Augustine (354–430), who in 381 was not yet a Christian.

Augustine – never accused of being an intellectual slouch – spent some fifteen years (400–16) laboring on his treatise *On the Trinity*. His concern was to warn the West of the dangers of tritheism. In the course of his work he commented: "Human speech at once toils with great insufficiency. Yet we say three persons, not in order to express it, but in order not to be silent." Again, the intent of doctrine is not to define the mystery of God but to confess it.

Jesus and Humankind: Christology

The development of the doctrine of the Trinity entailed Christological reflection in that every affirmation about Christ carried an understanding of the Trinity and vice versa. Now that the fourth-century church confessed the unity of God with the assertion of the divinity of the Son and Holy Spirit, questions arose concerning the relationship between divinity and humanity in the person of Jesus Christ. The New Testament authors had no doubt concerning the true humanity of Jesus – they had known him "according to the flesh" (2 Corinthians 5:16) – they had shared their lives with him. Yet, at the same time, the disciples were convinced that Jesus was not just another prophet sent by God, but rather that in Jesus, God met them in a unique and incomparable way. In some sense they were convinced that Jesus himself is divine; that Jesus had broken through the category of the prophetic. But how are the human and the divine related in Jesus? Does the divine Word replace the human mind or soul? A sense of the integrity of human nature criticized such a view on the basis that a person's soul and not merely his or her flesh must be saved through Christ. Furthermore, the locus of sin is not the body but the mind. As Gregory of Nazianzus (d. ca. 390), another Cappadocian bishop, succinctly put it, what is not assumed by God is not redeemed. Orthodox Christian tradition tended to oppose the Neoplatonic view that the spirit seeks the good but is imprisoned in a corrupt body. Gregory saw that it is the person's highest faculties that rebel. Therefore, if Christ has not assumed all of human nature, then not all of human nature is redeemed.

The Christological issue came to a head through Nestorius (d. ca. 451), the bishop of Constantinople, and his opponent Cyril (ca. 370–444), bishop of Alexandria. Here, too, of course, there were numerous non-doctrinal factors in the controversy leading to the councils of Ephesus (431) and Chalcedon (451) – rivalry between the theological schools of Antioch and Alexandria; jealousy of Alexandria toward Constantinople (Alexandria, long esteemed as the seat of learning and the bulwark of orthodoxy, was being overshadowed by the rise of Constantinople as the imperial residence); the power of monasticism; and the role of women.

The heresy associated with Nestorius, who had been a priest and monk in Antioch before becoming bishop of Constantinople – Nestorianism – basically held that there were two persons in Christ. However, it seems he did not actually teach this; and so like many heresies attributed to particular persons there is some inaccuracy here. The Antiochene emphasis upon the reality of Christ's human experiences of temptation and suffering led to the view that in Christ there were two persons in moral rather than in essential union. Since the Logos is eternal and only like can bear like, that which was born of Mary was the human only. The Incarnation was the indwelling of the Logos in a perfect man, as of God in a temple. In contrast, Cyril held the Alexandrian teaching that the divine and human natures were united in Jesus, who was God become man. Cyril's argument was that if Jesus did not suffer on the cross as the Word become flesh, his sacrifice did not truly bring salvation. In short, if only a man died on the cross, what is salvific about another victim of human cruelty?

When Nestorius became bishop of Constantinople he inherited a dispute over a title applied to Mary. Some insisted on calling her "theotokos," God-bearer or Mother of God, while others were calling her Mother of man. Nestorius, hoping for compromise, suggested that she should be called Mother of Christ ("Christotokos"), a term which he argued represented both God and man, as it is used in the gospels.

However, theotokos was a term that had become deeply rooted in liturgy and popular piety. In light of the formulation of Nicaea and Constantinople, the theotokos title expressed, especially for the Alexandrians, the belief that, in the Incarnation, deity and humanity were so closely united that neither birth nor death nor salvation could be attributed to one nature without the other. Alexandrian Christology used the liturgical term theotokos to support its emphasis on the unity of the person of Christ. To Cyril of Alexandria it was of course a natural expression. Indeed, it was used everywhere in the East except where the school of Antioch was influential.

Thus Nestorius' position ran aground on popular piety both in terms of the worship of Christ and the growing veneration for Mary. Furthermore, Nestorius, a powerful preacher, lacked discretion in using provocative phrases such as Mary could not carry God for nine months in her womb and God could hardly be wrapped in diapers. Cyril's counter-claim was to profess the unity of God with the man Jesus – it was God himself who was born, lived, taught, labored, and died in history. From Cyril's point of view, Nestorian Christology denied the affirmation that the divine Word truly became a human person, thus implying there can be no true redemption. Furthermore, for Cyril, the liturgical consequences of Nestorianism would mean that in the Eucharist only the body of a man would be resting on the altar, and this would rob the Eucharist of its life-giving power.

Nestorius also exhibited his inability to win friends and influence people by railing against the city's popular entertainments of circus races and theater; and demanding that monks remain in the monasteries rather than engage in public ministry. And he raised the question of whether the patriarch of Constantinople could overrule the patriarch of Alexandria. The "last straw" was Nestorius' confrontation with the emperor's sister, Pulcheria, who had dedicated her life to holy virginity.

Nestorius was certainly not the first – nor the last! – church leader who believed women should stay in their place. In his view, women who attended evening psalms and prayers as well as night vigils for the dead were inviting problems; so he locked women out of evening services. Nestorius then personally blocked Pulcheria from entering the sanctuary when, as her custom, she was to take communion with her brother and the priests, proclaiming that "only priests may walk here." She responded: "Why? Have I not given birth to God?" Nestorius drove her away with the incensed charge: "You? You have given birth to Satan!" As if this were not enough, Nestorius then cancelled a popular festival dedicated to Mary that had become an occasion during the liturgical year when virgins and religious women were honored. Mary was not the mother of God, claimed Nestorius, but only the mother of Jesus the man, Christ-bearer, not God-bearer.

The emperor called the Council of Ephesus to settle the theological question. Ephesus, however, was both a haven for adherents of Cyril's position and the ancient cult center of the virgin goddess Artemis/Diana that by now had been co-opted to the cult of the theotokos. Whether or not Pulcheria had a hand in choosing this site, the city was packed with pro-Cyril supporters and monks angry at Nestorius. To cap it all off, the council met in a church dedicated to the Virgin Mary. Nestorius was excommunicated, and Jesus was declared fully God and fully human. Jubilant women escorted Cyril from the meeting.

The reaction to Nestorianism led to monophysitism – a Christology that merged Christ's divinity and humanity into one entity (*physis*). The strength of the Monophysite orientation was in the areas of Syria and Egypt where strong Semitic roots of the faith militated against any suggestions that the person of Jesus might be divided. In contrast, the Greco-Latin churches were influenced by their roots in classical antiquity.

In response, the emperor called a council to meet at Chalcedon, on the eastern shore of the Bosphorus, opposite Constantinople. Its dogmatic decision was decisively influenced by a doctrinal letter written by the bishop of Rome, Leo I, known as "Leo's Tome." Leo insisted that in Jesus there are two natures complete in one person, God and man. How this can be, Leo leaves a mystery – which is perhaps Leo's greatest wisdom. Leo summarized briefly and succinctly the Christology of the West that in Christ there are two full and complete natures which "without detracting from the properties of either nature and substance, came together in one person." Leo argued that the unity of the two natures is essential for redemption. The mediator between God and humankind, Jesus Christ, had to be able to die (according to his human nature) and not to die (according to his divine nature). He further emphasized that the two natures of Christ have separate modes of operation but one always acts in unison with the other. This is the doctrine of the *communicatio idomatum* – in the unity of the person there is an exchange or "communication" of properties or attributes. It is therefore proper to say that the Son of God was crucified and buried or that the Son of Man came down from heaven. There is one indivisible God-man. Christ is to be acknowledged in two natures "inconfusedly, unchangeably, indivisibly, inseparably." The first two terms exclude Monophysitism and the last two exclude Nestorianism. The acclamation in response to Leo's proposal – "Peter has spoken through Leo" – enhanced the prestige of the bishop of Rome, and thus the eventual papacy rooted there.

The decision at Chalcedon was not an attempt to force the inexpressible into conceptual clarity. In the face of the endless discussions and controversies concerning the relationship of divinity and humanity in Jesus Christ, Chalcedon simply asserted that Jesus Christ is one person and at the same time he is truly God and truly man. The decision did not eliminate speculative questions, but it gave the questions a direction for speaking about the divinity and humanity of Jesus Christ.

The rivalry of the patriarchs of Constantinople and Alexandria brought grief upon both of them and allowed the eastern emperors to subject the church to their own authority. The Christological controversies enflamed the national passions of Egypt and Syria and fed the struggle for freedom from Byzantine overlordship. Monophysite bishops were placed in the sees of Egypt and Syria, thus eroding the unity of empire and church. Some scholars have suggested that this area of the empire was thus less able later to fend off Islam. Although subject to isolation and oppression, the Coptic Church in Egypt and its daughter church, the Ethiopian Church, have continued to today and are members of the World Council of Churches. Nestorianism also took root in Persia, from whence it sent missionaries to India and China. Another aftermath of these lengthy Christological controversies was the iconoclastic controversy that rocked the Greek Church in the eighth and ninth centuries. Here too there were non-doctrinal factors at play, such as the role and authority of monasticism, but the Christological issue was also present. The opponents of images argued that a representation of Christ's divine nature comes under the prohibition of images of God found in scripture. The proponents of images, on the other hand, appealed to the affirmation that the divine Logos did in fact become human.

Chalcedon's concerns were made known to the West in the so-called Athanasian creed that was cited at least partially for the first time by Caesarius of Arles (470–552). In 40 short statements it summarized the catholic dogma on the union in two natures of the person of Christ and the divine Trinity. But the Athanasian creed also contained a formulation that led to division in the church. It emphasized that "the Holy Spirit is from the Father and the Son, neither made nor created, but proceeding." This reference of filioque ("and from the Son") sought originally to emphasize that Christ is one essence with the Father. But it also stated that the Spirit proceeds in the same manner from the Father and the Son. This formulation distinguishes the creed from the usual emphasis of the Eastern theologians that the Spirit proceeds from the Father through the Son and is distributed over the whole creation.

That this formulation led to division between East and West lay not only in the different theological orientations – Eastern theologians started from the Trinitarian and Christological considerations of the unity of the Trinity, while Western theologians understood in their reflections that the Holy Spirit is the person uniting the Father and the Son. The early medieval Western insertion of the filioque into the Nicene-Constantinopolitan creed raised an essential point of contention between the Eastern and Western churches, that is, whether a part of the church could change by its own unilateral action the common confession of the church formulated by an ecumenical council. According to the Eastern church only an ecumenical council of the Eastern and Western churches could expand a confession that a council had determined. The controversy over the filioque in addition to other political and ecclesial tensions finally led to the Great Schism in 1054 between the East and the West. The East continues to view the addition of the filioque as a matter of schism while it is generally accepted in the West.

Chapter 4

The Heavenly City: The Augustinian Synthesis of Biblical Religion and Hellenism

The person in the West who more than any other put his stamp on the competing interpretations of salvation was St. Augustine (354–430), who also bequeathed to Western culture its penchant for introspection, pilgrimage, and alienation. No other theologian has been as influential upon the West as Augustine. He marked the theological–spiritual course for the church up to the modern period.

Aurelius Augustinus was born in Thagaste (in contemporary Algeria), a provincial bourgeois milieu. His father was a pagan and his mother, Monica, was a very devout Christian. Augustine lived in a time of great political and social crisis. By the time of his death while the bishop of Hippo Regius, a small North African seaport and Roman military post, the city was under siege by the Vandals. Aleric's Visigoths had pillaged Rome and shaken the Roman world to its foundations in 410, the symbolic date for the end of the Roman Empire in the West. The empire had been divided in 395. Whereas Byzantium, the Eastern Roman Empire, was able to defend its population, the defenses of the western half of the empire were too weak to withstand barbarian pressures. Indeed, Rome itself was no longer the capital of the empire. In 330 Constantine had established a new capital in the town of Byzantium strategically located in the isthmus between the Black and Aegean Seas, that he in all humility named Constantinople. By 404 Rome was no longer even the capital of the Western Roman Empire, having been displaced by the exarchate of Ravenna. These events marked a major break with the existing Roman Empire, and left a political vacuum that would be filled by the bishops of Rome. Next to the political and economic upheaval in Augustine's time there were also significant theological controversies threatening the unity of the church, in particular Donatism and Pelagianism.

Augustine lived in an afflicted society that appeared to be rushing pell-mell towards disintegration. "Eternal Rome" was collapsing as it faced perpetual warfare with barbarian war bands in the north and the challenge of Persia in the east. Taxation skyrocketed to finance the military; the poor were victimized by horrendous inflation; and the rich sought refuge in unparalleled accumulations of property. To add insult to injury for the Christians, the charge arose that all these disasters were the consequence of the abandonment of the traditional gods of the empire.

Augustine's family, though not rich, was free and he was bright. His father, Patricius, a minor official, perceived that economic advancement was through a classical education, and thus he scraped together the means for Augustine to gain such an education with its emphasis upon rhetoric. Hot tempered but generous, Patricius was admired by fellow townsfolk for his sacrifices for Augustine's education, yet Augustine himself makes only passing reference to his father's death. His mother, Monica, however, was convinced through a dream that he would be converted to Christianity. She followed Augustine relentlessly in pursuit of her vision of Augustine's conversion. Augustine himself seems to have realized that her devouring love had an element of "unspiritual desire" in it for in his *Confessions* he wrote: "She loved to have me with her, as is the way with mothers, but far more than most mothers."

Insight into Augustine's development is provided by his *Confessions*, written between 397 and 401. This book takes his story to the death of his mother in 387; in his unfinished *Retractions*, begun in 426, he corrects and discusses those aspects of his writings that he came to see were in error or were misunderstood.

Augustine's *Confessions* present his reflections on his family origins and development. Indeed, this writing is the means by which Augustine came to terms with his own history; it was an act of therapy for what we might now call a midlife crisis. Since 391 he had been forced to adjust to a new life-situation as a priest and then as a bishop. He received the latter responsibility against his will. His own plan for his life after his dramatic conversion to Christianity was to live in a monastic community apart from the world; but this desire had to be set aside. The ecstasy and optimism of his conversion was now sobered by increasing introspection into his past, into his sins, into his ability to function in his new ecclesiastical responsibility. Augustine felt he had to assess himself, and he did this by reinterpreting his past life as it led to his conversion. The *Confessions* are Augustine's effort to find himself.

This was an intensely personal period of adjustment for Augustine. In being thrust into the life of episcopal action he was not only losing his treasured life of contemplative withdrawal (John Calvin will have a similar experience) but was also now exposed to the spiritual temptations he thought he had escaped by renouncing in 386 his acclaimed public position as a rhetorician. He had rejected a life as a public figure because of its seductive dangers of ambition, desire for praise, temptation to dominate others, and the sensitivity to insult. Now he found himself faced once again by the hazards of pride in what he called "the puffed-up existence" of a bishop. All that had horrified him at his conversion was reappearing, never mind that it was now in service of the church.

Thus, immediately after his ordination as a priest, Augustine wrote a desperate letter to his bishop begging for time to retire and study scripture. Why? He was already an accomplished theologian. The actual life of a priest, he discovered, revealed his limitations. "I found it," Augustine wrote, "far, far more than I had thought . . . I just had not known my own powers: I still thought they counted for something. But the Lord laughed me to scorn and, by real experience, wished to show me to myself." As he put it later in his *Confessions*, the office of ministry bit into him and he was "made deeply afraid by the weight of his sins."

To face his ministry, Augustine worked through his past. His conversion alone was not enough to sustain him. He had to work through his emotions regarding the death of his mother, for example, and reached the conclusion that the idealized figure who had haunted his youth is finally just an ordinary person, a sinner like himself. Augustine could have cut himself off from his past – not an unusual reaction to a conversion experience. Instead, he called on his memory to understand his present. He dealt specifically with his feelings in relation to his personal growth and the nature of human motivation. Hence his account of stealing a pear is a paradigm for the sinful human condition. One would think that a cosmopolitan person like Augustine could have come up with a more lurid example! But, as he noted, it was not the pear he wanted to enjoy, but rather "the theft for its own sake, and the sin." He "derived pleasure from the deed simply because it was forbidden." He recalled how in his pagan life he had enjoyed crying at the theater, but had no reaction to the news of his father's death. In his reflections Augustine set the tone that will permeate medieval culture and theology up to the Reformation period and in many respects up to today. That tone is introspection.

Introspective self-scrutiny, seen in the *Confessions*, is the soul's longing for God, a longing to return to its maker, a longing experienced as restlessness, a pressing sense that in all things there lies something beyond, something that calls to God. The sense of not being at home in the world, the sense of alienation, is fundamental to Augustine. But of course it is not unique to him or to

Christianity. It is the Hellenistic tension between the transient and the permanent, the temporal and the eternal. It is what Plato expressed in the longing to escape the shadows of the cave and enter the sunshine of the intelligible world. It is even more clearly expressed by Plotinus, whose writings influenced Augustine. But in Augustine the longing for God is transposed from human restlessness to a response to God's love and condescension; it is, in the opening lines of the *Confessions*, the movement of the Holy Spirit in the human heart: "for you have formed us for yourself, and our hearts are restless till they find rest in you."

Augustine's experience is a transitory foretaste of the joys of heaven. Its transitoriness reminds Augustine and his culture – as if it needed reminding as the empire collapsed – of mortality and the destiny of death. The experience is also a way of ascent – both upwards and inwards – that passes beyond material things to the depths of the soul. Here is also Augustine's debt to Plotinus. Here too is reflected the changed context of Augustine's Christianity from that of pre-establishment Christianity – the enemy of the Christian is no longer the external persecutor but the internal tempter. While early Christians faced external pressures that at times led to martyrdom, the worst enemies of the Christians of Augustine's time were sin and doubt; the climax of a person's life would not be martyrdom but conversion from the past. That is why to Augustine's contemporaries the *Confessions* was a startling book. Their ideal was to present conversion as the beginning of a new life that leaves the past behind.

In contrast, Augustine regarded the past as alive in the person's present. Personal differences related to unique past experiences. His mother would have become a drunkard had she not been caught tippling at age six, and his friend Alypius' unsatisfactory experience of sex as a boy contributed to his chastity. Augustine explored the ability of persons to imprison themselves by their past. Thus he reflected on the theft of a pear as a paradigm of the limitations of human freedom and the proclivity to self-destruction. He described the bondage of the will as a chain of iron. Unlike so many ancient and medieval biographies where the heroes are described in terms of their ideal qualities, Augustine revealed his past and its grip on him. He made it clear that a person's past is very much alive in the present, and that no dramatic conversion experience should delude a person into believing he or she could easily discard a past identity.

Augustine's Path to Conversion

One of Augustine's first crucial concerns was the question of truth. Cicero's *Hortensius*, a work that summoned philosophy to the truth, influenced him as a student. He also tried reading the Bible, but thought it was an inferior writing compared to the works of the Latins. The next influence was Manichaeism, an Asian-Hellenistic religion somewhat similar to Gnosticism in its equation of good and evil with spirit and matter. The religion attracted Augustine because it provided a rational explanation of sin in terms of an ultimate principle of evil in the world fighting against the ultimate principle of good. The material world should be avoided by an ascetic discipline designed to free the soul from the matter that enmeshed it in evil. Manichaeism was a system of salvation in which truth is seen as saving truth. However, Augustine's disappointment in the intellects of leading Manichaeans he met, and his encounter with Neoplatonism and the church in the figure of Ambrose, bishop of Milan, led him to forsake this religion. Some, however, have suggested that the profound pessimism concerning created nature inculcated by Manichaeism influenced Augustine's later doctrine of sin.

Augustine's search for philosophical certainty was aided by his discovery of Neoplatonism. Instead of the forces of good and evil, Neoplatonism spoke of being and non-being. In this schema, evil is seen as a defect, a lack of being. Persons are pulled downward or direct their attention downward away from being toward non-being, and therefore are not what they ought to be. But as attractive as this was intellectually for Augustine, he was unable to put it into practice. Neoplatonism showed him the good, but did not enable him to reach it. He wondered how Christian monks, who to him were not very bright, could control themselves, but he with all his publicly acclaimed brilliance could not. Yet Platonic thought helped prepare him for acceptance of the gospel. It was, Augustine says, God's design that he read the Platonists before the scriptures.

The other major influence was the church in the person of Ambrose of Milan, a brilliant rhetorician who had embraced Christianity and then been acclaimed bishop. Ambrose exhibited in his own person to Augustine that he did not have to sacrifice his intellect to become a Christian. A further impetus to conversion was the story recounted by his countryman Ponticianus of the conversion of two of his friends on reading Athanasius' *Life of St. Antony*.

In his *Confessions* Augustine recounts his conversion as a highly emotional event. He withdrew into his garden and flung himself down under a fig tree, weeping for release from the anger and judgment of God, and heard a child chanting: "Take up and read; take up and read." Interpreting this as a divine command, he opened the Bible and read the first passage he saw, Romans 13:13–14: "Let us live honorably as in the day, not in reveling and drunkenness, not in debauchery and licentiousness, not in quarreling and jealousy. Instead, put on the Lord Jesus Christ, and make no provision for the flesh, to gratify its desires." Instantly, his gloom and doubt vanished.

Augustine's Theological Contributions

Augustine's contributions to Western theology and church history are legion. Most noteworthy are his grounding of Christian faith in the concept of love, and his responses to the challenges posed in his time – and ever after – by Donatism and Pelagianism.

Augustine attempted to subsume Christianity as a whole under the aspect of love. Christianity is purely and simply the religion of love. He articulated this motif so powerfully that it became axiomatic for Roman Catholic and much of Protestant theology to affirm Christianity is a religion of love.

Augustine's mother tongue was Latin, thus the word he used for Christian love is *caritas*, the word from which we get "charity." Caritas in Augustine's sense is primarily love to God made possible because God first loved humankind. Love to God is the central virtue; all other virtues are expressions of it. With this theological orientation Augustine is free from all legalistic ethics. Only love is enjoined upon the Christian; where love is, no other requirements are necessary. Hence, Augustine's famous ethical injunction: "Love God and do what you will." Caritas is the root of all that is good; its opposite, the root of all that is evil, is *cupiditas*, the word from which we get "cupidity" and also "Cupid," the Roman god of love. Both caritas and cupiditas are terms for love. The difference between them is that caritas is directed to the sole true and real possibility for happiness, God; whereas cupiditas is (mis)directed love toward things assumed to provide happiness but which are only transient. Both terms refer to "love" but are polar opposites – caritas ascends to God, Being itself; cupiditas descends to inferior beings and then nothingness. Augustine's fundamental assumption – gained from his acquaintance with Neoplatonism – is that all love is acquisitive. That is, persons desire what they believe will fulfill them. In short, Augustine perceives that the eudaemonism – the drive for fulfillment – of ancient philosophy has apologetic value. Everyone wants to be happy. By linking love closely to the desire for happiness, Augustine finds it possible to regard love as the most elementary of all manifestations of human life. There is no one who does not seek his or her happiness. For Augustine this is synonymous with the claim that there is no one who does not love.

Here is the foundation for the theology of ordered love that will develop in medieval scholasticism. Anything may be an object of good *for me* – thus even in evil the person loves nothing other than what he or she thinks is his or her good. Creatures, being incomplete, always desire their completeness.

This leads to consideration of the opposition between loves, between caritas and cupiditas. Cupiditas is sin because it is misdirected love; it is love directed to inferior objects; it is curved down toward the earth rather than toward God. But God is above us, and thus we are to direct our love upward toward the good that is God. Earthly goods confuse us, and drag our love downwards toward them. Cupiditas then is the search for the good, which while good, is nevertheless incapable of providing final satisfaction. Here again we see the influence of Neoplatonism. Being itself is the highest good; to turn away from the highest good, from Being, is to turn toward non-being. Augustine was thus using Hellenistic philosophy to express to his audience the biblical view that sin is not just breaking rules or laws but breaking relationships by turning away from God and the neighbor, breaking the chain of being. Since only God is the highest good, the immutable good, only God can give persons complete fulfillment. When love is directed to lower goods in the search for fulfillment it then becomes idolatrous, it mistakes the creature for the Creator; by loving perishable goods, sin is a turn or perversion toward privation and death.

The distinction between true and false love raises the question of Augustine's understanding of the creation. He rejected Manichaeism with its denigration of the material world, and he affirmed the goodness of creation because it is God's creation. Hence love of the creation is not in itself sin if this love is rightly understood. He clarified this by making a distinction between enjoyment (*frui*) and use (*uti*). Frui is the love that "enjoys" its object, whereas uti is the love that "uses" its object. The analogy Augustine used to illustrate this distinction is that of a voyage to our homeland. The ship is "used" as a means to get us to our home that we "enjoy." But the danger is that the voyage may so appeal to us that we forget home and enjoy the trip to the extent that it becomes an end in itself.

The earthly city is not the true home of the Christian, but rather the vehicle (the ship) for our travel to our true home in the heavenly city. The world, our earthly city, is given as a means and vehicle for our return to God; it is to be used, not enjoyed. The world, if enjoyed, drags us down and away from God. In his theology of history, *The City of God*, Augustine wrote: "Accordingly, two cities have been formed by two loves: the earthly by the love of self, even to the contempt of God; the heavenly by the love of God, even to the contempt of self. The former, in a word, glories in itself, the latter in the Lord." The issue in the succeeding history of Western Christendom became whether this disjuncture is spiritualized toward an ascetic otherworldliness or understood as the critical perspective for life in this world. One major aspect of the Augustinian heritage was an emphasis upon Christians as pilgrims in an alien land. In Augustine we find the themes of pilgrimage and alienation that become so influential in Western Christendom and culture. The motif of ascent to God will be illustrated in art and literature by images of the ladder to heaven. To be sure, Augustine emphasized that human ascent to God depends first of all upon God's descent to humankind; the descent of Christ enables human ascent to God.

Augustine and Donatism

Donatism was a movement concerned for the moral purity of the church, especially its ministry, and as such has been a perennial occurrence in the history of the church, especially in relation to renewal movements such as the Gregorian reform (eleventh century), Reformation radicalism (sixteenth century), and modern charismatic movements.

In the African Christianity of Augustine's time, the purity of the church was a central concern. To the Donatists of North Africa, however, the moral purity and holiness of Christianity had been severely compromised by the failure of nerve of many of its members, including priests and bishops, during the major persecutions. In 303 the emperor Diocletian launched a major attack, the "Great Persecution" (303–5), upon the church. Churches were destroyed, Christians were forced to hand over their sacred writings, bishops and congregational leaders were arrested and forced to make sacrifices to imperial divinities.

During this and prior persecutions numerous Christians had witnessed to their faith to the extent of losing their lives. Moved by these martyrdoms, pagans had joined the church; hence the famous phrase "the blood of the martyrs is the seed of the church." Not all Christians, however, when confronted by the choice of torture and possibly a grisly death or renouncing their faith, chose the former. Bishops who opted for the better part of valor were known as "traditors" because they "handed over" the scriptures to the authorities. After the persecutions subsided, there were "traditors" or "collaborators" who wished to rejoin the community. We can imagine the mixed emotions of those who had remained steadfast at great cost. At any rate, it was believed by the Donatists that those bishops who had handed the scriptures over to the authorities had thereby deprived themselves of all spiritual power.

It was believed that Caecilian, bishop of Carthage, had been ordained by a traditor. Thus, in 311, 80 Numidian bishops declared his ordination invalid and elected another bishop in his place. The new bishop was soon succeeded by another bishop named Donatus. Hence arose the "Donatist party."

Caecilian held on as bishop. The case of the Donatists was perceived as weak because some of them also had been traditors. And the rest of the Latin church was more open to tolerating past collaborators. Furthermore, Constantine wanted a unified and respectable church. Since Caecilian was the existing bishop,

Constantine supported him against what appeared to non-Africans as exaggerated and parochial grievances.

Division was hardened by military persecution of the Donatists. When Julian the Apostate was emperor (361–3), tolerance was renewed for the Donatists and the Catholic party was attacked.

Augustine's response to the Donatists was influenced by the fact that he became a Christian in Milan, not in North Africa. In the former context the major issues were philosophical and cultural rather than the generations of rancor about purity in North Africa. To Augustine, the Donatists threatened the universality and unity of the church by their advocacy of isolation for the sake of purity. Whereas the Donatists regarded their church as an alternative to society, a place of refuge like the biblical ark, Augustine believed the church should become coextensive with human society as a whole and thereby transform and perfect the bonds of human relations.

The questions sharpened by the Donatist controversy were whether the church is defined by the purity of its ministers or the catholicity of its sacraments; whether the church is "in" society or should separate from society in order to live the faith; whether the church is a community of saints and sinners or the company of the pure. What is the source of the true unity of the church?

Already at the Council of Arles (316) under the influence of Constantine, the principle was decreed that ordination and baptism are not dependent upon the worthiness of the administrant. Augustine continued this principle with the argument that the holiness of the church is due to the divine presence in it in the sacraments. In other words, the message is not dependent upon the moral character of the messenger. If the contrary was held, then the gospel would always be in doubt because the hearts of the ministers cannot be read. The Word of God and the sacraments are valid whether or not the minister runs off with the choir director or even contemplates doing so in the future. Hence the Conference of Carthage (411) affirmed that salvation depends upon God, not humankind. The Donatists were not won back to the church, but were condemned. One of the historical consequences was that Augustine turned to the power of the state to repress the Donatists by appealing to the parable of the banquet in Luke 14:16–23 that ends with the mandate: "compel them to come in." Thus the emperor Honorius around 400 applied heresy laws against schismatics. Throughout the history of the church Donatism has been a temptation that can also take the form of a congregational Donatism that claims that the truth of the church depends upon the moral purity of the assembly rather than Word and sacrament. The Donatist party was concerned that the church would forsake its prophetic critique of culture and succumb to moral complacency, whereas the "Catholic" concern was that Donatism would lead to moralism and sectarianism.

The Pelagian Controversy

Augustine had been involved with the Donatist controversy for nearly fifteen years (396–411), but that did not deter him from continuing theological reflection on the problems of evil and salvation. His own conversion experience naturally led him in the direction of emphasizing the absolute priority of divine providence for salvation. He rejected any suggestion that persons could make the smallest step toward righteousness before God without divine assistance. Thus, well before the Irish monk Pelagius (355–420) appeared on the scene advocating human freedom to choose righteousness, Augustine through his personal experience and intense study of the Bible held that humankind was a *massa peccati*, a "lump of sin," since the fall of Adam, with no merit of its own. Indeed, he held that sin was passed on seminally from Adam. The sense of original sin as the original sexually transmitted disease was derived from his (mis)reading of Romans 5:12 as "In whom, that is, in Adam, all sinned." Augustine did not read Greek and depended on a Latin translation of the second century that rendered the Greek as *in quo omnes peccaverunt* ("in whom all have sinned"). The *in quo* was read in the masculine by Augustine to mean "in Adam." Sin therefore is universal and inevitable since all humankind descended from Adam. What was at stake for Augustine in this reasoning was the affirmation that redemption depends solely upon God, since all are sinners. Humankind cannot depend upon any natural capacity for salvation; salvation is received, not achieved. The downside of Augustine's interpretation of the universality of sin as hereditary has been a suspicion about sexuality.

Pelagius, however, heard Augustine to be advocating fatalism. Augustine's dictum in his *Confessions*, "Give what you [God] command, and command what you will," clearly appeared to Pelagius to jeopardize human morality. He and his followers were already concerned that now that Christianity had become the established religion, people were entering the church for convenience or political and economic advantage rather than as disciples. As Søren Kierkegaard, nineteenth-century critic of the Danish state church, would later charge, when everyone is a Christian no one is a Christian.

Like the Donatist party, the Pelagians were also interested in perfection. Pelagius called upon Christians to live out their faith in perfection. Certainly, grace was necessary for humankind because the power to be good had been weakened by Adam's fall into sin. But baptism gives forgiveness, and Christ has provided a new law and example to guide humankind toward perfection and the consequent eternal reward. Pelagius believed that Christians through divinely provided free will and through God's law could carry out Christ's commands as laid down in the New Testament, and thereby live a virtuous life. Pelagius neither admitted original sin nor original fall. A person's sin is his or her own. Adam was certainly a bad example, but he did not infect the whole human race.

Pelagius preached repentance with great zeal. To an insecure age with a "pull-yourself-up-by-your-bootstraps mentality" comparable to American ideology, such moral exhortation was well received. By 418 Pelagius was joined by impressive champions of his views, including the bishop of Eclanum, Julian. Their theology emphasized the freedom of the human will. The rationalist strain here is apparent with the argument that since God has given us the law, it must follow that we have the ability to do it. Centuries later during the Enlightenment, Immanuel Kant would phrase this: "You ought, therefore you can." Since we have free will, it is possible for us to decide for or against the good. Christ would not have commanded divine perfection had he known this was beyond achievement (Matthew 5:48: "Be perfect, therefore, as your heavenly Father is perfect"). The Old Testament law and the Sermon on the Mount emphasize our responsibility to God's command. Human difficulties in fulfilling the law are removed by grace. The law is further supplemented by the teachings and example of Christ; thus God's assistance may be seen as instruction through moral example.

To Augustine the tendency to identify grace with the exemplary life and moral teaching of Christ displaced Christ's atoning death and perverted the good news into bad news, a new legalism that placed the burden of proof for salvation upon human effort. Furthermore, the assumption that humans have the capability to fulfill the law of God would lead to naive optimism.

In 417 pope Innocent I (reign 401–17) took the side of Augustine against Pelagius in a way that contributed to the growing power of the Roman bishop, later expressed in the phrase: *Roma locuta, causa finita* – "Rome has spoken, the case is closed." In 418 the Synod of Carthage confirmed the condemnation of Pelagianism, and variations on its theme of human free will in relation to salvation were condemned at the Synod of Orange in 529. Like Donatism, however, Pelagianism has a perennial appeal and continually crops up in the history of Christianity.

In the last decades of his life Augustine wrote two of his greatest works, *On the Trinity* and *The City of God*. The former is a brilliant exposition of the doctrine that seeks to free it from the metaphysical puzzles that had beset the East since the Council of Nicaea. Augustine presented the divine quality of love binding the three persons of the Trinity descending to humankind as the creative force of forgiveness by which God recreates his own image in each sinner. The *City of God*, begun in 411 and completed in 426, responded to the questions of whether the fall of Rome and other disasters were the consequences of the imperial establishment of Christianity. Were the neglected gods of old Rome taking vengeance? In this theology of history, Augustine rejected such views and also set forth a schema of church–state relations. The earthly images of the two cities are the church and the state. But the earthly church is still not the city of God; and the state is necessary to preserve peace and human righteousness. Augustine presented the two cities as ideal types, even though these were reflected in earthly governments according to the purpose of their existence. Thus the state too could reflect divine purpose.

Augustine presented a whole theory of society that drew upon classical culture yet also consciously criticized it. Here too he was a great influence upon the medieval church and culture that, under his influence, would continue to aspire to the city of God. In the Augustinian theology of history the problems of human society relate to sin, and thus even the virtues of humankind are but "splendid vices." Therefore no political and social system can make people good. The best that government can do is to provide enough peace to enable the pilgrimage to the heavenly city to continue. Augustine also attacked in his theology of history the classic cyclical view of history, the endless wheel of the pagans. The church's mission is to convert and transform society. In this, the goal is not withdrawal into purity but engagement with the world. The medieval church clearly took this to heart.

Chapter 5

The Development of Medieval Christendom

The church may indeed in Augustine's eyes be a reflection of the heavenly city, but he also recognized it existed in the earthly city. Vital to the church's existence in the world was its developing institutional structure as it expanded outward from the collapsing Roman Empire into the lands it would shape to become what we call Europe. The institutionalization of the Augustinian aspiration to the city of God that formed the foundation and then shaped the contours of medieval Europe included a number of often simultaneously interweaving factors, through which ran the red thread of imperial–papal relations. The warp and woof of this tapestry of medieval development included the authority of the bishop of Rome; the Roman cultural heritage of jurisprudence and language; the barbarian invasions that eroded imperial power and left the church as the major integrating force in the West; the rise of monasticism as a missionary movement; and the two-pronged evangelization of the Continent from the south by Roman missions under Gregory the Great and from the north by Celtic missions from the British Isles. The temporal parameters of this complex development are the papal reigns of Gregory the Great (590–604) and Gregory VII (1073–85).

Monastic life exerted such influence that its significance is almost impossible to overestimate. The monastery provided a glimpse of order in the midst of the prevalent disorder of early medieval life so marked by dearth, disease, and death. It was a place for penitence, for refuge, for protection, and above all for the worship and collective prayer to obtain God's favor in the combat against sin, death, and the devil.

Monasticism was rooted in one of the most cited passages of the Middle Ages: "What must I do to inherit eternal life? . . . sell what you own, and give the money to the poor . . . then come, follow me" (Luke 10:21ff.; Matthew 19:16ff.; Mark 10:17ff.). Monasticism was the liturgical and spiritual "exercise"(Greek: *askesis*, "exercise," "training," also asceticism; see Mark 8:34) in the battle against sin. A characteristic mark of monasticism was separation from the world. Its early form in the East (Palestine, Syria, Asia Minor, and Egypt) was hermitic marked by self-denial and seclusion. Ironically, the extreme asceticism of hermits often attracted visitors and then disciples. Thus there arose a form of religious communal life first advanced by Antony (d. 356) and Pachomius (d. 346) in Egypt that became the dominant form of Western monasticism. Life in a community, strictly controlled by the abbot ("father"), was gradually formalized by rules. An early rule for Byzantine monasticism was that of Basil of Caesarea (ca. 330–79); in the West the Rule of St. Benedict of Nursia (ca. 480–ca. 560) dominated the development of "Benedictine" monasticism.

In addition to the crucial recitation of psalms and prayers in eight daily services, the monasteries provided pastoral care, homes for "surplus" noble children, education, preservation of classical culture, promotion of civilization, and evangelization.

Monasticism initially entered Europe via southern Gaul. Many bishops and even popes such as Gregory the Great came from the ranks of monks, and close ties between monastery and diocese promoted monastic expansion. Most important however for the thriving of monastic culture was the patronage provided by kings and nobles. In return for their support, founding families and donors were remembered in the prayers of the monks. Medieval religion thus has been described as "the living in service to the dead." The nobles who built churches and monasteries assumed they could install the clergy in them. Noble support was of course crucial for these foundations, but at the same time their view of the church and its activities as their own property created tension down the line with the papacy, and set the stage for the struggles between pope and emperor that culminated in the Investiture Controversy.

Roman monasticism was rivaled by Irish–Scottish monasticism with its rigorous penitential discipline and missionary drive, derived from its orientation to ascetic wandering for the sake of Christ represented by Colomba (ca. 521–97), founder of the Iona monastic center of missions. The major wave of missionaries to the Continent consisted of Anglo-Saxons affiliated with Rome after the mission to Britain impelled by Gregory the Great in the seventh century. The rigorous piety of the Irish monastic church and the organizational strength of the Roman church were epitomized in the missions of Winfried (Boniface, 672–754). He worked on the Continent organizing churches, closely tying his work to Rome and the papacy; and also relating classical culture and Christian piety, thereby creating the groundwork for the so-called "Carolingian Renaissance." After a fruitless mission to the Frisians in 716, Pope Gregory II sent Boniface to the German peoples. After a second journey to Rome where he rendered an oath of obedience to the pope, he returned to Germany and was active from 723–32. Upon his third journey to Rome (732), Gregory III made him an archbishop. During a final mission to the Frisians he received the perfect ending for a saint – martyrdom! He is buried in his church in Fulda.

The cultural and educational work of the church and especially the monasteries related initially to the reality that whole peoples were brought into the church by actions of kings or nobles who upon conversion forced mass baptism upon their people. Missionary work thus began mostly after baptism. The use of Latin as the church's language created a cultural–intellectual unity that was a significant aspect of medieval culture. The cloisters were centers for education where ancient wisdom was collected in "florilegia" (anthologies). The pedagogical role of monasteries extended beyond collecting wisdom to promoting it through writing and copying. Such work was deemed meritorious for salvation. Hence the story that a sinful monk saved his soul because God cancelled a sin for every letter he copied; and fortunately, he had just one remaining letter to his credit.

Monastic culture was not limited to copying texts from the past, but also engaged in a variety of intellectual pursuits related to monastic life. These included maintaining a liturgical calendar; mathematics for managing estates; calculations for determining times of prayer, readings, and manual labor; legal work related to monastic estates; histories and biographies of founding monks and their monasteries; rhetoric for preaching; theological and philosophical reflection concerning the Bible and tradition; art for adorning manuscripts with exquisite miniatures, places of worship, vestments, liturgical materials and vessels; music for worship; and architecture. Inspired by the biblical description of the construction of Solomon's Temple (1 Kings 5–7), magnificent churches were built to honor the saints and worship God.

The Emergence of the Papacy

The papacy developed from unassuming beginnings to become the most significant institution of Western Christianity. Beginning with collegial relationships, the office of bishop – guarantor of apostolic truth – gradually developed in the direction of a monarchical office. In Rome the claim to be an apostolic church rested upon the tradition of its founding by the two most significant apostles, Peter and Paul. The Roman church also benefited from its political and cultural significance as a world capital, and its noteworthy charitable activities. By the later fourth century the Petrine basis of the papacy was generally acknowledged in the Roman environs, but lacked a "documentary" basis outside the New Testament promise that Peter will be the rock on which Christ will build his church (Matthew 16:18ff.). Early documentation for a "foundation narrative" came around 500 with the translation and embellishment of a second-century Greek document, the "Epistle of Clement." Purported to be a letter by Clement I to James, the brother of Jesus, it claimed that Peter himself passed his authority to Clement before a gathering of the Roman Christian community. The document thereby affirmed the institution of succession by claiming a historical link between Peter and the Roman line of bishops, and its use of the head and body metaphor contributed to the monarchical claim of the papacy.

Pope Leo I (r. 440–61), himself a superb jurist, used Roman law to clarify the relationship of successive bishops to Peter. Inheritance law stated that the heir legally took the place of the dead person, including estate, assets and liabilities, and rights and duties. The pope thus became Peter's heir in regard to his powers though not his personal merit. Leo expressed this juristic point with the formula of the pope as "the unworthy heir of St. Peter."

Leo further developed papal primacy with the argument that Christ founded a new society for which monarchical government was given to Peter and then inherited by Peter's successors. This is the beginning of the concept of a Christian commonwealth or society (corpus Christianum). The difference, Leo argued, between the papacy and the empire is that the papal monarchy was the result of a unique divine act, whereas the imperial monarchy was a historical development of human organization and administration and therefore divinely willed only in a secondary sense. Leo enhanced his theoretical argument through the prestige he gained by his "Tome" presented at the Council of Chalcedon, and by his convincing Attila and later Geiselich not to pillage Rome in 452 and 455.

Leo's program reached its classical formulation under pope Gelasius I (r. 492–6). The Gelasian theory, sometimes called the "Great Charter of the Medieval Papacy," distinguished sacred power from royal power by use of the Roman distinction between legislative and executive authority. To Gelasius, the authority of the church was legislative, while the authority of the secular ruler was executive. In Roman law legislative authority was above executive authority. Thus Gelasius both distinguished church and state – in order to keep the emperor out of church affairs – and at the same time implied that the church as legislative institution gave power to the emperor as executive. Here is the legal formulation of the position stated earlier by Ambrose of Milan: "The emperor is in the church, not above it."

Needless to say, emperors were not enthusiastic about these developing positions. Indeed the emperor Justinian (527–65) turned Gelasian theory on its head, claiming that the emperor as legislator was "divinity walking on earth." The consequent imperial program to reduce the Roman bishop to the level of an imperial appointee, along with other tensions, led the Roman church to turn to the West. The person who epitomizes this shift is Gregory the Great, often called the father of the medieval papacy.

Gregory was of aristocratic descent, thoroughly trained in Roman law, and had been a papal ambassador to the court in Constantinople. Aware that Rome would be little able to dent imperial ideology, Gregory was already prepared to turn to the West when he became pope in 590. Thus Gregory intensified papal activities in Spain, Gaul, and Britain. His vision was to unite these areas into a Christian commonwealth under the Roman faith. His policy bore fruit in papal dealings with the Franks.

By the mid-eighth century, the Frankish Merovingian house had declined to the point that the government was being run by the mayor of the palace, Pepin the Short, who exercised royal authority on behalf of the crown and was contemplating a coup. Pepin approached the papacy for support through the famous missionary Boniface. Pope Zacharias (r. 741–52) responded that he who ruled should be king. With this sanction, Pepin became king in 750. In 751 he was anointed by archbishop Boniface – the first anointing of a Frankish ruler.

Meanwhile the political situation in Italy was deteriorating. In 751 the Lombards drove the imperial garrison from northern Italy and expelled the imperial representative from Ravenna, the seat of Byzantine rule in the West. Pope Stephen II (r. 752–7) perceived that the Frankish monarchy could be a means for extricating the papacy from Lombard pressure and imperial control from Constantinople. In 754 Stephen met and negotiated with Pepin for the restoration of papal lands taken by the Lombards in exchange for papal prohibition of the choice of a Frankish king outside the family of Pepin. At St. Denis in 754 the pope anointed Pepin as patrician of the Romans, thereby designating him regent and protector of Italy. The charisma of blood, the hereditary Merovingian line, was now replaced by the charisma of divine grace conferred by the pope upon a usurper king.

Pepin fulfilled his promise by crushing the Lombards and donating the lands to St. Peter and thus to the papacy in a solemn document deposited at the tomb of St. Peter – the "Donation of Pepin" (756). Thereby the papal state was created that would last for more than the next 1,000 years. The emperor in Constantinople was not pleased! The papacy, however, found precedent in the "Donation of Constantine." The Donation of Constantine was a novelistic product that portrayed Constantine being healed of leprosy by his baptism by the pope. The grateful Constantine then proclaimed the pope and his successors to be forever over all other bishops, and then gave the pope the imperial crown and all the imperial territory in the West with the right to create consuls and patricians. The pope, not a greedy fellow, retained only Italy as a papal patrimony, returned the imperial regalia to Constantine, and allowed him to establish a new seat of government in Byzantium. The legend served a number of vital papal interests. It explained the establishment of Constantinople in 330 as the new capital of the empire as a direct result of papal permission; it established the papacy's secular prerogatives; and by the return of the imperial insignia to Constantine, it established the papal right to create the emperor by crowning him. In 1440 the Italian Humanist Lorenzo Valla exposed the Donation of Constantine as an eighth-century forgery.

It was Pepin's son, Charlemagne, who from his accession in 768 fully lived up to the crucial role of patrician of the Romans. He added more territory to the papal patrimony, and carried forth a marked Romanization in religious matters. He also came to the rescue of pope Leo III (r. 795–816) when local Roman nobles tried to depose him.

Charlemagne agreed to go to Rome in support of Leo in his quarrel with the Roman nobles, who by now had charged him with lechery and perjury. Leo cleared himself of the charges by taking a solemn oath on the basis that the pope could not be judged by anyone (see 1 Corinthians 2:15). This principle had first been set forth in the early sixth century in the so-called Symmachan forgeries that included the decree: "Nobody can sit in judgment on the first (apostolic) see which distributes rightful justice to all. Neither the emperor nor the whole clergy nor kings nor people can judge the supreme judge."

At this time, Christmas 800, Leo took the initiative to crown Charlemagne Roman emperor in a highly orchestrated event. Prior to the celebration of the Christmas mass – held for a change at St. Peter's rather than the customary Santa Maria Maggiore because of the pope's awareness of Frankish veneration of Peter – Charlemagne had agreed to take the title of emperor. While Charlemagne was kneeling at the altar, Leo came up behind him and placed a crown on his head. The carefully coached crowd responded: "Charles, most pious Augustus, crowned by God, great and peace-loving emperor, life and victory!" The function of universal ruler – as certainly intended by Leo – meant that the East would no longer be considered the legitimate Roman Empire, for it was now "translated" to the West. Leo thereby extricated the papacy from the East, and placed the center of the Christian world in Rome rather than either in Constantinople or Aachen, Charlemagne's capital. This was the birth of the Holy Roman Empire as a religious, geographical, and political phenomenon.

Papacy and Empire

The Carolingian church prospered under Charlemagne. As the authority and power of the bishops and archbishops increased, the lower clergy looked to the papacy as a source of unity and court of final appeal. They desired a strengthening of the papacy not for its own sake but as a means of checking both the growing secular control of the church (the proprietary church system wherein clergy were appointed by secular lords and kings) and as a restraint upon the autonomous behavior of the archbishops. It was this circle of the lower clergy that developed the Pseudo-Isidorian Decretals, a mid-ninth century collection of doctrine and laws attributed to the Spanish archbishop Isidore of Seville (560–636). The papal ideology expressed in this collection was not new, but the laws fabricated to support these concerns were. A recurrent theme throughout the Decretals is papal primacy with the concomitant emphasis upon the Roman church as the mother of all churches; the head from which all jurisdictional and governing authority and power flows.

The first pope to make full use of the Pseudo-Isidorian Decretals was Nicholas I (r. 858–67), the most effective pope between Gregory I and Gregory VII. According to Nicholas, the pope is Christ's vice regent on earth and speaks with the authority of God. Papal decisions have the force of law, and councils are only the means for carrying out papal decrees. No one may sit in judgment on the pope, not even the emperor. This exalted claim led Nicholas to oppose both Frankish and Byzantine rulers. Since spiritual authority is higher than secular authority, the church must at times exercise direct influence over the state, but not the reverse, for the state exists to support the church. Nicholas saw in the Pseudo-Isidorian Decretals the power for creating a homogeneous Europe under Roman papal authority. His skill and genius in pursuing his goal may be seen in three cases: the marriage affair of Lothair II, king of Lorraine; the Hincmar case; and the Photian Schism.

When Lothair became the king of Lorraine in 855 he was married according to German law to Waldrada, who bore him three children. The opinion of the time was that German marriages were dissoluble. After becoming king, Lothair married a noblewoman, Theutberga, in a lawful Christian marriage. When it appeared she would remain childless, Lothair wished to put her aside and take back Waldrada. The archbishops of Cologne and Trier supported the king, as did two papal legates at the Synod of Metz. The papacy, however, came out strongly in favor of the Christian marriage and declared Theutberga his legal wife. The consequences were the displacement of Germanic marriage custom, the unprecedented deposition of two archbishops and the threat of excommunicating the king.

The Hincmar case involved the powerful archbishop of Rheims, who had excommunicated bishop Rothad of Soissons for refusing to accept a ruling by the archbishop. Rothad appealed to the papacy on the basis of the Pseudo-Isidorian Decretals. Nicholas then forced Hincmar to reinstate Rothad as well as other deposed clerics.

The Photian Schism provided the opportunity for Nicholas to assert papal rights in the East. The complicated – indeed, truly Byzantine – context included the deposition of the patriarch Ignatius of Constantinople for his refusal to commune the immoral imperial regent, Bardas. Bardas then appointed a learned layman, Photius (ca. 820–ca. 897), to take the place of Ignatius as patriarch. Ignatius appealed to the papacy, but Nicholas' legates joined in approving Photius. Nicholas then repudiated his legates and declared Photius deposed. Photius replied in kind, and for good measure added the charge of heresy to the Western church for adding the filioque to the creed. The fortunes of Ignatius and Photius continued to go up and down in relation to Byzantine intrigues, but what is important in terms of the development of the papacy is Nicholas' conviction that the papacy had authority over the East, and the consequent separation of the Eastern and Western churches.

The Gregorian Reform

With the death of Charlemagne in 814 rule passed to his son Louis the Pious (r. 814–40), who divided the reign with his three sons, Lothair, Pippin, and Louis. Carolingian power however was now under assault both internally and externally. Sibling rivalry is an understatement for the constant conflicts among the brothers whose striving for power was abetted by the self-interest of semi-royal dukes. Further serious disruption was caused by Viking, Magyar, and Saracen invasions. In 843 the Treaty of Verdun split the kingdom in three, and the death of the last Carolingian, Louis the Child, in 911 facilitated the reassertion of tribal duchies.

Henry, Duke of Saxony (r. 919–36), revived the German monarchy and the Carolingian ideal of empire and its unity with the church. The expansion of the realm under his son Otto the Great (r. 936–73) used the church for political goals, a policy that also preserved the church's holdings. Otto's vigorous assertion of royal authority over the church expressed not only his ambition but also his devotion to advance the church's ideals, culture, and civilizing mission. Otto nominated bishops who for the most part had been trained in the royal chapel; as bishops they received royal support that extended even to jurisdiction over serious criminal cases. From the time of Otto III (r. 983–1002) even whole counties with all their rights were bestowed on episcopal sees and royal abbeys. The financial benefits included not only lands but also profits from tolls and markets. These Ottonian privileges laid the foundation for episcopal territorial power. At the same time, the imposition of clerical celibacy meant that the clergy could not pass on power and wealth, but only receive it from the kings.

The bishops also received the symbols of their office – ring and staff – from the rulers. Otto would hand the crozier to the newly appointed bishop or abbot with the words, "receive the church." Such investiture was possible because the king was not simply a layman. His anointment as ruler, at that time regarded as a sacrament, raised him to the sphere of a vicar of Christ. Thus an anointing formula from Mainz presented the king as a participant in ecclesiastical office and an intermediary between the clergy and the people. Again we are reminded of the importance of liturgy – here utilized in the establishment of political legitimacy. Otto III, Henry II (r. 1002–24), and Henry III (r. 1039–56) all took this theocratic ideal very seriously. The downside was that bishoprics were filled with men who had reason to be loyal to the monarchy, and rulers began to think they were responsible for reform of the church.

Otto the Great's increasing hegemony over other nations pointed to the goal of imperial anointing and coronation. Since this presupposed the possession of Italy, the Saxon dynasty focused its politics on the conquest of the Lombard kingdom. Otto's motives – as mixed as political goals are – were also formed in a political and religious climate that blended aspirations for royal power and a renewed empire with Christian universalism and the awe of the sacred transmitted in an imperial anointing.

In 951 Otto I assumed the crown of Italy, but Pope Agapetus II refused him the imperial crown. In 961 Pope John XII appealed to Otto for protection, and in return Otto was crowned Roman emperor in 962. John XII intended that Otto serve the church as its military protector – an ornamental copy of the Donation of Constantine was presented to Otto – but Otto had his own aspirations. He had the papal enemies he conquered swear allegiance to him instead of the pope. The pope was enraged and instigated a revolt in Rome. Otto put down the revolt, deposed the pope (963), and appointed a layman as successor, Leo VIII (r. 963–5). Otto then inserted into the papal oath of election an oath of obedience to the emperor. Termed the "Ottonianum," this remained the basis for numerous imperial interventions in papal affairs for nearly a century.

Barely had Otto left Rome when John XII returned, expelled Leo VIII, and took vengeance on his adversaries with the help of the Romans. The pope died soon after this, allegedly from a stroke after being caught in bed with a Roman's wife. Benedict V succeeded him but was exiled by Otto, who reinstalled Leo VIII.

The Ottonian line ended with the death of Otto III in 1003. The Ottonians had succeeded in renewing the empire of Charlemagne. In the north, east, and southeast the Poles, Hungarians, and Bohemians formed nations whose churches were oriented toward Rome. Farther east, the Russian church was under the influence of Byzantium. In the eleventh century Denmark, Norway, and Iceland were also Christianized, and in the twelfth century so too was Sweden.

A fundamental turn in the relationship of the papacy and the empire came from the monastic reform movement associated with the Cluny monastery. Cluny struck a spark of hope for the late ninth-century world of Viking-devastated monasteries and an enfeebled papacy seemingly intent on wading deeper and deeper into moral and political swamps. Cluny was founded in 910 in Burgundy on land given by Duke William of Aquitaine, the Pious. The charter affirmed that Cluny was to be self-governing under the protection of the pope. The abbot had the right to choose his own successor and thus insure continuity. Its lands were to be secure from all invasion or secularization. And the Benedictine Rule as interpreted by the Benedictine reformer,

Benedict of Aniane (ca. 750–821), was to be strictly observed. The Cluny movement quickly spread throughout France and Italy. Cluny itself progressed from an example emulated by other monasteries to the exercise of direct control over other monasteries. By the beginning of the twelfth century there were more than 1,500 monastic houses tied to Cluny whose heads were appointed by or responsible to the abbot of Cluny. Cluny also became the most renowned center of liturgy and ecclesiastical splendor of the time.

The Cluniac reform movement caught fire with the nobles as well as the monastics and prompted the laity to expect increasingly higher standards of the clergy. The German king Henry III (r. 1039–56) was deeply religious and impressed by his duties as a Christian king. So, for example, in 1043 he proclaimed a "day of indulgence" forgiving all his foes and urging his subjects to do likewise. His contemporaries sometimes viewed him as a monk in worldly garb because of his piety and delight in participating in processions and dedicating shrines. His support for Cluny was related not only to his piety but also to the fact that his wife was the daughter of William of Aquitaine. Henry was not unique among the rulers of his day; Edward of England was called Edward the Confessor, and throughout Europe nobility and rulers were building churches and endowing monasteries. Monastic intercession was viewed as a key to heaven, and it was not unusual for nobles to spend their last days in a monastery and desire to be buried in monk's garb.

Cluny expanded its concern for monastic reform to the reform of all clerical life. By the 1050s the reform movement was focused on two issues: simony and Nicolaitanism. Simony (Acts 8:18–24) was the giving or receiving of clerical office for money or other considerations. Nicolaitanism (Revelation 2:6, 14–15) was the breach of clerical celibacy. The most explosive issue was simony, viewed by the Cluniacs as any lay investiture in clerical office.

A noted exponent of Cluniac reform was the monk Peter Damian (1007–72), later cardinal bishop of Ostia. An orphan from a poor family in Ravenna, Damian rose to a comfortable life and then suddenly at 29 resolved to become a monk. He entered the Benedictine monastery at Fonte Avellana and soon excelled at study and a rigorous asceticism that might appear to us as self-torture. He wrote a biography of the ascetic St. Romuald (c. 950–1027) and after being chosen abbot introduced Romuald's Rule, which emphasized asceticism. Each psalm recited was to be accompanied by 100 lashes on the bare back. The whole Psalter was equal to 15,000 lashes – those were the days when it paid to be a slow reader! The practice became a craze and led to the Flagellant movement. Damian insisted on separation from the contemporary world, which he denounced as worse than Sodom and Gomorrah, and he never tired of railing against simony, clerical marriage, and clergy bearing arms. He became the spiritual counselor and censor of seven reform popes, and called himself "lord of the pope" and Hildebrand's "holy Satan." He died in 1072, just a year before Hildebrand became pope Gregory VII.

The degeneracy of the papacy at this time stirred Henry III to reform it. Between 955 and 1057 there were 25 popes, 12 by imperial appointment and the rest by the Roman aristocracy, five of whom were deposed by emperors – hardly an affirmation of the claim that the pope could be judged by no one. In 1046 Henry entered Italy and called for a synod that met at Sutri where he had pope Sylvester III deposed and Gregory VI exiled, and then made a German bishop, Suidger of Bamberg, pope Clement II. From Henry's perspective his coronation gave him authority to bestow symbols of ecclesiastical office and order the affairs of the church, including the appointment of three popes, all men of high caliber and all Germans (Clement II, Leo IX, Nicholas II). Henry's choice of Germans was not in order to incorporate the papacy into the German church but to insure reform by independence from the Roman nobility. The preliminary condition for renewal was a free papacy; this Henry accomplished by recourse to the old imperial right of participating in the papal election established by the Ottonianum. Ironically, Henry's papal choices ushered in an age of papal reform that turned against imperial intervention.

Among the popes named by Henry, Leo IX (r. 1048–54) was the most significant. Leo brought the spirit of monastic reform into the papacy, thereby strengthening it and the entire church. Leo regularly held synods at which simony and clerical marriage were condemned, and he laid the groundwork for the College of Cardinals. Two men from this circle were especially important for the further development of the papacy, the monk Humbert (d. 1061), later cardinal bishop of Silvia Candida, and the Cluniac monk Hildebrand (ca. 1033–85), later pope Gregory VII. Humbert was a master of literature and law, especially the Pseudo-Isidorian Decretals. He pushed for the abolition of the proprietary church system and condemned simony and concubinage.

The strengthened papacy under Leo IX conflicted with Byzantium when he asserted papal primacy over southern Italy, an area claimed by Constantinople since the eighth century. The patriarch of Constantinople, Michael Cerularius (r. 1043–58), refused to accede to the papal claim. The ante was upped when the patriarch closed the Latin churches in Constantinople and took over the few Latin monasteries. Humbert attacked the patriarch with fiery and passionate claims, including the Donation of Constantine. Escalating tensions included further points of conflict such as the mission to the Slavs and the filioque. Humbert then led a legation to Constantinople and on July 16, 1054 laid a papal decree of excommunication on the high altar of St. Sophia. The patriarch returned the favor, and the Eastern and Western churches were now in open schism.

The Investiture Conflict

Humbert gave the starting signal for the Investiture Conflict in 1057 with his three books against simony (*Adversus simoniacos*), defined as any participation of a layperson in the conferral of ecclesiastical office, thus condemning lay investiture. The insignia of the office of bishop (staff and ring) could only be given by one who himself held this office. In 1059 a Roman Synod, presided over by pope Nicholas II, issued a papal election decree that precluded the right of the German king to introduce an election proposal.

The monk Hildebrand as pope Gregory VII (r. 1073–85) reiterated laws against simony and Nicolaitanism in synod after synod. He summarized his convictions in his *Dictatus Papae*, a list of 27 chapter headings for a projected collection of canon law. These sentences, largely mined from the Pseudo-Isidorian Decretals, presented the most important primatial rights and were to guide reform. Significant among them are that the pope "alone has the power to depose emperors"; "that no general synod may be called without his order"; "that his decree can be annulled by no one, and that he can annul the decree of anyone"; "that he can be judged by no one"; "that the Roman Church has never erred and will never err to all eternity"; and "that he has the power to absolve subjects from their oath of fidelity to wicked rulers." He based these rights upon Matthew 16:18ff., Augustine's *City of God*, and the claims of Gregory I and Nicholas I. Gregory, never renowned for flexibility, became exceedingly rigid on the matter of secular investiture. Clerics were forbidden under pain of excommunication and annulment of the completed action to accept from a layperson the investiture of bishoprics, abbeys, and churches; the investing layman would also be excommunicated.

When king Henry IV (1056–1106) invested the archbishop of Milan, a man whom the papacy did not even know, Gregory sent Henry a letter of admonition. Henry himself declared on the basis of his authority as Protector of the Romans that Gregory had forfeited his papal authority and must resign. Gregory's response was to suspend Henry from governing, annul oaths of loyalty to him, and excommunicate him. This prompted the German princes to form an alliance against Henry in order to advance their own interests. Gregory, however, wanted Henry's obedience not his head, and provided a compromise that forestalled the election of a new king so long as Henry promised obedience and penance. This is the setting for the famous confrontation at Canossa, the fortress of countess Matilda, a strong supporter of Gregory. For three days in January 1077 Henry stood bareheaded and barefoot in the snow outside the castle. Within the castle, Matilda as well as abbot Hugh of Cluny, Henry's godfather, implored clemency. In the end, Gregory could not refuse his priestly office and received Henry back into the Christian community. In the history of the German kingship, Canossa was such a profound humiliation that the phrase "nach Kanossa gehen" (to go to Canossa) came to mean "to eat humble pie."

The investiture struggle ended with a compromise between king Henry V and pope Callistus II in the Concordat of Worms (1122): the king renounced investiture with ring and staff, but retained investiture with the scepter before the vows. That the Concordat of Worms did not finally settle tensions between church and state is evident in England in the struggle between king Henry II and Thomas Becket, archbishop of Canterbury (d. 1170). However, the Gregorian reform movement reflects the appeal of churchly ideals and the concomitant growth of lay religiosity in the tenth and eleventh centuries. This in turn created increasing demand that the clergy should be superior in piety and morality. The ideological struggle arising in this context pushed the papacy to strive for the sort of distinctiveness and freedom from state control that in turn led to papal efforts to negate the sacramental power of kingship and to dominate secular rulers.

The Crusades

The ascetic and penitential revival stimulated by the Cluniac movement and the increased power of the papacy found an unwholesome outlet in the crusades. Penitential pilgrimages to Jerusalem had occurred for centuries and continued after the Muslim conquest of the city in 638, for Jerusalem was considered a joint shrine for Christian and Muslim. This changed with the rise of the Seljuk sultans (1055–1194), whose armies defeated the Byzantine army in 1071 and captured large areas of Asia Minor that had been a source of wealth and manpower for the Roman Empire of the East. Over the next centuries the Byzantines would periodically appeal for help from the West, only to discover the truth of the adage "with (Christian) friends like these who needs enemies."

The Byzantine emperor, Alexios I Komnenos (r. 1081–1118), petitioned the papacy for help. It was a call that found an enthusiastic echo in the Western church, whose increased self-consciousness in the time of Gregory VII supported the conviction that the holy places should be rescued from the hands of unbelievers. The long held sense of pilgrimage combined with the concept of forcible mission and conversion since Charlemagne and the church's ethos of the "Christian knight" formed the background for the enthusiastic response to pope Urban II's call for a crusade at the Synod of Clermont in 1095.

Urban spoke of the suffering of Christian pilgrims and the desecration and destruction of holy places, and called upon Western Christendom to combat Islam and liberate the Holy Land. Urban sweetened the pot with the promises of spiritual and temporal rewards – a plenary indulgence, earthly treasures, the diversion of feuding into combat against a common enemy, and political and economic expansion. The mixed motives of the crusades and crusaders are reflected in archbishop William of Tyre's (ca. 1130–ca. 1187) *History of the Deeds Done Beyond the Sea*: "Not all of them, indeed, were there on behalf of the Lord . . . All of them went for different reasons."

Whatever the reasons, the series of crusades lasting to the final Turkish victory in 1244 left bloody tracks as so-called crusader states were established and fell, Constantinople was sacked by the Western "Christians" who went to rescue it, and various efforts such as the "children's crusade" of 1212 went horribly wrong (thousands of children died or were sold into slavery). The crusades did not permanently conquer the Holy Land nor did much to impede the advance of Islam. They exacted a great toll in life and treasure, and whatever idealistic spirit impelled them degenerated into savage conduct. Crusader attacks on the Byzantine Empire severely damaged East–West relations and contributed to the ultimate triumph of the Ottoman Turks in 1453. The sense that a military crusade for the Prince of Peace is an oxymoron began to be recognized before the crusades petered out. Also, the church's need for funds in order to finance the crusades led to criticism of the church's turn from apostolic poverty.

The crusades did strengthen the role of the papacy, and gave rise to military orders – the Templars, the Hospitallers or Knights of St. John, and the Teutonic Order – that continued to play important roles in Europe, and brought nobles into service of the church. The crusades also stimulated the trading cities of northern Italy and their influence. Along with the rise of trade, the drain on feudal lands and properties made possible a new political role for towns, and the rise of a "third estate," the bourgeoisie, especially in France. Knowledge in the West was greatly expanded by contact with the East, and led to an intellectual awakening. The soil was prepared for the later Renaissance as Europeans rediscovered the classics, became interested in history and literature, and supported the development of universities. These streams flowed into the marked theological development of the Middle Ages: scholasticism. The crusades also stimulated the demand for relics and indulgences. The encounter with non-Christian culture called into question the universality and uniqueness of the church, and stimulated theological reflection.

Chapter 6

Faith in Search of Understanding: Anselm, Abelard, and the Beginnings of Scholasticism

The early period of scholasticism, so-called for its systematic use of reason utilized in the schools, stretches from the eighth century to the twelfth. The critical investigation of the received tradition and its authority is the essential beginning of scholasticism.

Medieval intellectual life was nourished by the Bible and the Augustinian heritage transmitted to the West by Gregory the Great. Efforts to collect and transmit the classical heritage and the theology of the church fathers were furthered by Charlemagne and the so-called Carolingian Renaissance. In 782 he recruited the most renowned scholars of the day, Alcuin of York (ca. 735–804) and Theodulf of Orleans (ca. 750–821), to improve the Frankish monastic schools and to raise the educational level of the court. Alcuin, former master of the cathedral school at York, established Charlemagne's palace library as well as a library and school in Tours, and promoted instruction in the works of Boethius, Augustine, and Latin grammarians. Theodulf, a leading theologian and poet of the time, wrote treatises on a number of theological subjects, including a defense of the filioque; his hymn "All glory, laud, and honor" continues to be sung today as the Palm Sunday processional. At court, Charlemagne surrounded himself with learned and zealous churchmen whose advice he sought and sometimes followed. Charlemagne himself was said to understand Greek and Latin, although he could not write. When in 794 Charlemagne decided to make Aachen his capital, he conceived of it as a new Rome, a center not only of political and administrative power but also of learning and the passing on of knowledge. He proceeded to establish new schools, to patronize scholars, and to mandate study in all monasteries and bishops' houses under the rubric "let those who can, teach." The preservation and dissemination of classical learning in these schools and monasteries is the source of much of the classical literature in the West.

With few exceptions, organized study in the tenth century depended upon monasteries and cathedral schools. Cathedral schools, so-called because they were connected to cathedrals, did not have the regulated life of the monastic schools and included boys not dedicated to the clerical life. In addition to similar concerns with regulating the liturgy, the cathedral schools were engaged in correspondence and business transactions. By the eleventh century there appeared to be a growing intellectual restlessness, evident in the willingness of students to go most anywhere for the sake of learning. By the mid-twelfth century it was clear that students knew where they wanted to go to study, and that they knew their studies would have market value in relation to the growing bureaucratic and economic needs of royal courts and cities. These students then created a demand for more teachers, and the eventual creation of universities.

The extent of the growing Carolingian political and educational self-consciousness is manifest in the *Libri Carolini* (The Caroline Books, ca. 791), themselves a testament to the revival of learning in the West. The occasion for the *Libri* was the iconoclastic controversy in the East. The Byzantine Empire, under pressure from Islam and the growing power of its own monks, had tried to dampen the fervor of both by limiting the use of icons, especially on the outside of churches. The theological rationale advanced by the imperial party was that since icons represented only the humanity of Christ, they either divided Christ's unity like the Nestorians or confounded it like the Monophysites. The persecutions and social unrest in the wake of emperor Leo III's 726 edict that images must be destroyed led to the Second Council of Nicaea (787) led by the new patriarch of Constantinople, Tarasius, in concert with the empress Irene and attended by papal legates. The council defined and restored the veneration of icons.

The Franks learned of the iconoclastic controversy and then received a faulty translation of the Acts of the Second Nicene Council from pope Hadrian I. The Frankish response in the *Libri* condemned the Second Nicene Council, thinking it had enjoined adoration of images equal to that due to God. The non-doctrinal factors affecting the composition of the *Libri* included general Frankish dislike for the Byzantines, and Charlemagne's own irritation with the empress Irene. In 794 Charlemagne presided over a synod at Frankfurt attended by all the Frankish and English bishops, and two legates of the pope that responded to the "heresy" of Second Nicaea. Hadrian, however, refused to withdraw his recognition of the Nicene assembly or to obey Charlemagne's demand that the Byzantine emperor be excommunicated. Apart from the political and theological conflicts here, we see the increasing self-confidence in learning and appropriating the theological tradition in the West, and an additional impetus toward the separation of the churches of East and West.

Universities and Scholasticism

The Carolingian concern for education lived on in the great schools of Aachen and Tours, hence the term "scholasticism" for the knowledge of this time occurring expressly in the schools. The basis for formal education, directed almost exclusively to the clergy and monks, was the classical Roman focus on the liberal arts (the subjects thought appropriate for a *liber*, a "free" man). The basic three, the *trivium*, were grammar, rhetoric, and dialectic. It should be noted that *the* language of education was Latin; thus all students began their education by learning this foreign language. The *trivium* was supplemented by the *quadrivium*: geometry, arithmetic, astronomy, and music. The "higher" professional studies were theology, law, and medicine. The intellectual capital of the medieval world consisted basically of the Bible and the church fathers, supplemented by the work of Boethius (d. 524), whose ambition was to preserve and present Greek learning to a Latin world rapidly being driven back on its own resources. The medieval excitement and enthusiasm for schools may be elusive to the modern mind. Thanks to the polemics of the sixteenth-century reformers and intellectuals, the medieval era in general and scholasticism in particular has received a bad press. The bias that scholastics were more interested in intellectual parlor games than "real life" continues with the old question that always arises when scholasticism is mentioned – "how many angels can dance on the head of a pin?" Historically, however, there is no doubt about the flesh and blood character of the leading intellectuals as they wrestled with the realities of their day.

Anselm (1033–109), known as the "father of scholasticism," left his home in northern Italy after quarreling with his father and set off in search of knowledge. He ended up in northern France at the monastery of Bec because of the intellectual renown of its prior, Lanfranc (ca. 1005–89), a fellow Italian called in 1070 by William the Conqueror to become archbishop of Canterbury. Anselm stayed on at Bec, became a monk at the age of 26, and gained renown as a teacher. The last 16 years of his life were in public political service as the archbishop of Canterbury, a position forced on him against his will. The English king, William Rufus, not renowned for his piety, had kept the see vacant in order to use its funds, but upon becoming very ill and fearful of eternity he hoped to make amends with the church by appointing an archbishop. Anselm, on a visit to England in 1093, was seen by the local bishops and the king's councilors to be the ideal candidate, but Anselm refused the honor. So the councilors and bishops literally carried Anselm off to the church with the bishop's staff pressed against his closed fist. Anselm wrote to his brothers at Bec: "It would have been difficult to make out whether madmen were dragging along one in his senses, or sane men a madman, save that they were chanting, and I, pale with amazement and pain, looked more like one dead than alive." The king survived his purported mortal illness only to be assassinated a few years later. Before that, however, Anselm went into self-imposed exile because the king continued to exploit the church and resist Gregorian reform measures.

The other great contributor to scholasticism, Peter Abelard (1070–1142), had an even more colorful life. The eldest son of an educated knight, Abelard became a knight errant of the mind, willing to go anywhere in search of his holy grail, knowledge. An exceptionally brilliant youth with an ego to match, Abelard trekked off to Paris to study with reputed scholars whom he soon dismissed as without substance. For example, jealous of the attention paid to theologians, Abelard sought out the illustrious Anselm of Laon (ca. 1050–1117), whom he then described as a barren tree – all leaves and no fruit. After disagreeing with some of the Paris Masters, Abelard began his own lectures in competition, and attracted their best students. Abelard's lack of the better part of valor was also evident in his affair with Heloise, the brilliant and comely niece of his fellow canon at the Cathedral of Notre Dame. Engaged to tutor her in philosophy and Greek, Abelard soon became engaged in extracurricular activities and she became pregnant. The rage of her guardian led to a gang attack on Abelard that in his words "cut off those parts of my body with which I had done that which was the cause of their sorrow." That event also cut short his teaching career at Paris. Having incurred the wrath of his teachers and colleagues, Abelard next incurred the wrath of ecclesiastical authorities with his book on the Trinity that he was himself forced to consign to the flames at the Council of Soissons in 1121. To round things off, angry monks chased Abelard from his monastery because he had argued that the patron saint of the monastery was not Dionysius the Areopagite, companion of St. Paul. Abelard aptly titled his autobiography, *The History of My Calamities*. For Abelard, academics was clearly neither an ivory tower nor a spectator sport.

Abelard certainly disturbed the guardians of the old order – recall that a generation earlier Gregory VII and his colleagues had condemned clerical incontinence. But Abelard's danger was not that he slept with a woman, but that his life and theology were an expression of a new understanding of love arising in twelfth-century southern France and making its way north. Romantic love – celebrated by troubadours and expressed in the poems and songs of courtly love – was a new idea of love destined to take over Western ideas until its banalization in Hollywood movies, "true confessions" journalism, and "bodice-ripping" novels. To Abelard and to Heloise, the relationship of individuals should trump the oppressive institution of marriage. Indeed, it was Heloise who did not want the marriage pushed on her by Abelard. "God knows," she later wrote to him from her nunnery, "I never sought anything in you except yourself; I wanted simply you, nothing of yours. I looked for no marriage-bond, no marriage portion." Heloise shared Abelard's low view of marriage, a view transmitted to their time from the early church fathers such as Jerome and Augustine. They also shared the "ethic of intention" set forth in Abelard's *Scito te ipsum* (Know Thyself). So Heloise wrote to him: "It is not the deed but the intention of the doer which makes the crime, and justice should weigh not what was done but the spirit in which it is done." They both thought marriage could add nothing to their relationship, but would rather detract from it by interfering with Abelard's intellectual work. So Abelard wrote: "What man, intent on his religious or philosophical meditations, can possible endure the whining of children . . . or the noisy confusion of family life?"

It may be suggested that Abelard's experience of the love of Heloise – with both its heady joy from which he composed love songs, as well as its profound pain and loss – was influential upon his understanding of the atonement, sometimes called an anthropocentric theory of the atonement. The significance of the Incarnation now is not in satisfying the claims of either Satan or God, but rather in the example and teaching of love manifest in Jesus, and the renewed love of humankind for God and others that Jesus' example stimulates. The monastic and feudal inspirations of Anselm's theology are displaced by worldly and humanistic inspirations in Abelard. As already noted, the guardians of the old order were not ready for that kind of subjectivity.

The major excitement of the time however was not the lives of the academics, but logic! Logic became the exciting discipline, for it was an instrument by which it was thought order could be imposed on a chaotic world. The world was a realm of natural and supernatural forces, demonic and otherwise, over which persons had little or no control. The realms of politics and economics – even more so than today! – were similarly dis-ordered and intractable to thought. But logic – however weakly at first – began to open a window to an orderly and systematic view of the world. The whole process of simplification and arrange-ment was a revelation of the powers of the mind and provided a sense of order residing behind a bewildering complexity of appar-ently unrelated facts. From the end of the tenth to the end of the twelfth century the digestion of Aristotle's logic was the greatest intellectual task. By the thirteenth century, the curricula at Paris and Oxford made Aristotelian logic the main feature of under-graduate studies.

There were various steps and turning points in the develop-ment of scholasticism, including the development around 1200 of universities as a higher form of the school with the ideal of ordering knowledge into a coherent whole, the *summa*. The expansion of knowledge created a new organization of teaching and scholarly apprenticeship the purpose of which was, above all, to pass on the accumulating body of knowledge. Over time, there arose awareness of contradictory elements in the tradition and the necessity for responsible explanation or reconciliation of such conflicts. From this developed the critical examination of tradition by the use of reason. The critical relating of reason and the authority of tradition is essentially the beginning of scholasticism as a methodological phenomenon. Medieval scholasticism, then, is a methodology that received the classical heritage and theology of the church fathers, above all Augustine, and treated it with the help of dialectics and logic. The distinction of early, high, and late scholasticism is only a construct to aid discussion. The turning points are associated with distinguishable degrees of dealing with the classical heritage, especially of Aristotle. Early scholasticism is the period from 1000 to 1200. A new level of development appears from about 1150 as Aristotle's logical writings become known. High scholasticism begins about 1200 as the West became acquainted with the whole of the Aristotelian corpus, including his ethics and metaphysics, mediated through Arabic and Jewish writings. At the same time there arose the first universities in Europe in Bologna, Paris, Oxford, and Cambridge. The University of Paris, developing from the cathedral schools in the twelfth century, received its foundation charter in 1200, and by 1213 had a curriculum that included theology, canon law, and medicine along with the liberal arts. Pope Innocent III recognized the University of Paris as a corporation under the jurisdiction of the papacy in 1215. In 1257 it received an endowment from Robert de Sorbon, hence the Sorbonne. In Italy the Investiture Controversy stimulated Matilda of Tuscany to endow a school for the study of law that became the University of Bologna. Bologna then became famous for the study of canon law through Gratian's *Decretum* (1140), and added a theology faculty in 1360. The University of Naples was the first to be founded by royal charter (1224) to train state officials.

Contributions of Early Scholastic Theology

It is important to note that the use of reason for the critical analysis of the tradition was not the autonomous use of reason, unbound by authority and free of faith, that is the characteristic ideal of modern reason after the seventeenth and eighteenth-century Enlightenment. Reason, as understood by Anselm and his contemporaries, is theonomous reason, that is, it is rooted in God and is a gift to humankind. Anselm thus saw faith – indeed, prayer – as the foundation for the right use of reason; hence his famous expressions *credo ut intelligam* ("I believe in order to understand") and *fides quaerens intellectum* ("faith seeking understanding"). His emphasis upon meditation liberated theology from his day's slavishness to the arranging and harmonizing of past authorities; the task of science is not merely to repeat the words of others but to inquire and examine the data. He presented his rational proof for God in two writings. In the *Monologion* he set forth the later so-called cosmological argument for the existence of God on the basis of the appropriateness and order of creation. In the *Proslogion* he presented the so-called ontological argument for the existence of God: the idea of God is given in reason which holds that nothing greater than God can be conceived. Even the fool who says there is no God (Psalm 14:1) understands this statement. What is understood must exist in his understanding. But that than which nothing greater can be conceived cannot exist merely in understanding, for then it would not be that than which no greater can be thought. For it is greater to exist in fact as well as in the mind. Thus, God must exist in reality, not just in the mind, because otherwise God lacks being. Although this argument has been criticized on various grounds since Anselm proposed it, it continues to fascinate logicians and philosophers.

In his *Cur Deus homo?* (Why Did God Become Human?) Anselm presented a new theology of redemption through his theory of satisfaction. The Incarnation of God is not only conceptually possible but also conceptually necessary. Anselm's understanding of sin posits that sin is an objective deprivation of the honor that belongs to God. The decisive concept of the honor of God reflects Anselm's feudal social world. To deprive a person of his or her honor was a fundamental crime against the social order. Furthermore, such an offense is proportionately magnified according to the status of the person in the hierarchical order and therefore the satisfaction of the offense is also magnified. An insult to the king is far more serious than the same insult to a fellow peasant. If the maintenance of a king's honor was necessary for the preservation of his kingdom, of a baron's honor for his barony, and so on down the social scale, how much more infinitely important for the preservation of the entire social world, indeed, the cosmos, was the maintenance of God's honor. God's honor is so profoundly violated by sin that punishment must be exacted to satisfy God's honor. For God merely to forgive the offense of humankind would vitiate his justice and honor, thereby undermining the stability of the universe itself. For God to reclaim his honor by just punishment of humankind's offense would annihilate all humankind. The honor of God can only be restored by its satisfaction, which God himself does by becoming a human being and himself satisfying the offense of humankind, thus maintaining both God's honor and mercy.

Anselm's "satisfaction" theory of the atonement has also been described as theocentric because he located the satisfaction of God's honor within God himself. Anselm's theory not only reflects his feudal society, it also moves beyond the religious thought of prior generations that posited Satan's legal claim on humankind. Since the "cosmocentric" theory of the atonement advanced by Gregory the Great and earlier by Gregory of Nyssa (ca. 330– ca. 395), the atonement had been viewed as a cosmic struggle between God and Satan. The imagery, dependent upon the Chalcedonian formula that Jesus is fully God and fully human and stimulated by the verse in Job 41:1 ("Can you draw out Leviathan with a fishhook?"), is that Satan claims Jesus with the mistaken assumption that Jesus is just another mortal. Satan is fooled by Jesus' humanity (the bait) and hooked by Jesus' divinity when he tries to devour Jesus.

It was Peter Abelard who most famously promoted the dialectical method in his work *Sic et Non* (Yes and No). Aware of the contradictions within the received tradition, Abelard pointed out that the truth of the church is not simply given but must always be sought. This was a milestone on the road leading away from unexamined reliance upon past authorities. The way to the truth leads through inquiry and doubt. With the help of philological criticism and logical arguments the tradition is worked over in order to balance its contradictions and to find the abiding truth. *Sic et Non* is the first comprehensive exposition of theology as a science rather than as a meditation or a compilation of past authorities. Abelard proposed a series of 156 doctrinal questions with citations from the church fathers in support of both a "yes" and a "no" to each of them. He then proposed a critical methodology for determining the authenticity, reliability, intention, and historical context of the text in question. When resolution of the contradiction by these means was not possible, then the strongest witness with the greatest support was to be preferred. This method became obligatory for the whole of scholasticism.

The drive to impose order on the tradition was carried forth by Peter Lombard's (ca. 1100–60) *Libri quattuor Sententiarum* (Four Books of Sentences), which gave the opinions of different authorities on the basic theological topics of God, creation, fall, redemption, sacraments, and eschatology. Lombard's *Sentences* became one of the all-time bestsellers and remained the basic textbook for theology into the sixteenth century. The monk Gratian of Bologna achieved a similar ordering of the tradition in the realm of church law with his *Concordantia discordantium canonum* (*Concordance of Disconcordant Canons*, 1140). The so-called *Decretum Gratiani* was a foundational text for generations of law students and judges. The supplements to Gratian's work were published with his *Decretum* in 1582 as the *Corpus Juris Canonici* (Code of Canon Law).

Not all of the leading intellectuals of the time were enamored of the new scholastic method, however. Bernard of Clairvaux (1090–1153), the monastic reformer and mystic, self-appointed judge, jury, and prosecutor of Abelard, turned against rational criticism and the dialectical method. For him the presupposition for theological work is not rational knowledge but rather the humble adaptation of the human will to the divine. It is ironic that Bernard, who hounded Abelard with inquisitorial fervor, himself refined further than Abelard the introspective conscience that Augustine bequeathed to the West. Born into a noble family, Bernard by the age of 22 persuaded 30 other young noblemen, including his brothers, to join the Benedictine renewal movement that had recently developed an order in its own right, the Cistercians (named after its foundation in Citeaux). The rigor of the Cistercians had already brought the order to the edge of extinction when Bernard's impact so transformed it that it came to be known as the Bernardines. Bernard has been called the "uncrowned ruler of Europe" because of his multifaceted influence on the election of popes, politics of kings, preaching of crusades, reforms of the church, and pursuit of heretics. But above all it was his promotion of mystical piety that secured his fame, then and now. Thus Dante (1265–1321) presented Bernard in the *Divine Comedy* as the representative of mystic contemplation who leads him to the Virgin Mary in Paradise.

The meditative literature that flowed from the Cistercians under the dominating influence of Bernard emphasized personal experience, appealed to the individual conscience, and plumbed the spirit of humankind. In a sense, this was scholasticism experienced, for it did not reject the age's love of logic but shifted it to the self-conscious, systematic search of the soul. Ascent to God was posited in the progress of self-knowledge, and presented in terms of logical steps of an intelligible development beginning with self-love and moving through self-knowledge to union with God. Logic was used to investigate the internal movements of the soul and states of mind. This "psychologizing" of theology is already present in Bernard's reworking of Benedict's treatise on the 12 steps of humility.

Bernard's tremendous spiritual influence resided not only in the power of his personality and perception but also in the readiness of his age to look inward, a readiness that also informed and received Anselm's emphasis upon meditation and Abelard's call to know oneself. The humanism and romanticism of this so-called "twelfth century renaissance" was graphically expressed in its changing art. Images of the crucifixion shifted from representations of divine power and majesty to depictions of extreme human suffering. The heroic images of Christ the King, a crowned and royally clothed warrior on the cross with head erect and open eyes expressing power, slowly changed to images of a humiliated, dishonored man, eyes closed, whose head and arms slump under the pain, and whose naked body shows his wounds. Among Bernard's many hymns still sung in Protestant and Catholic churches today, the new sensibility of the twelfth century comes through in his "O sacred head, now wounded, with grief and shame weighed down, now scornfully surrounded with thorns, thine only crown." Likewise, the images of Mary and the child Jesus once depicted as Mary the God-bearer (theotokos) and Jesus as a miniature adult, right hand raised in benediction, left hand clasping a symbol of dominion, were now transformed into the image of a helpless baby at Mary's breast. Maternal tenderness and infant vulnerability began to come to the fore, and Marian piety blossomed in the universities into heated arguments about the Immaculate Conception. The stage was being set for the Christian romance incarnated in St. Francis. Anselm's faith seeking understanding, Abelard's quest for self-knowledge, and Bernard's love seeking spiritual union will in the person of Francis focus on the symbolism of the wandering homelessness of the beggar, "naked following the naked Christ." The virtue of poverty will be transmuted from the Benedictine renunciation of pride to the romantic embrace of material impoverishment.

Chapter 7

The Medieval Church

Between the tenth and fifteenth centuries the medieval church responded to an array of issues ranging from the number and meaning of the sacraments to the challenges of a developing urban culture and economy. The papacy, recovering from its earlier weakness, realized the aspirations of Gregory VII's "Dictates" in the papal reign of Innocent III, only to find its earthly rule curtailed by the conflict between pope Boniface VIII and the French king Philip the Fair and the consequent rise of conciliarism.

The Cultural and Theological Development of the Sacraments

Medieval humankind at the mercy of natural and social forces largely beyond its control and understanding sought security, peace, and order. Thus in liturgy, art, architecture, political and religious thought, and piety, people strove to create an image of an eternal world within a world of change. The image of the city of God on earth was developed in terms of the biblical image of the Christian community as a body (e.g., 1 Corinthians 12; Ephesians 4; Colossians 3), the corpus Christianum. By the tenth century the functional social expression of this "Christian commonwealth" was parsed into three "orders" or "estates": peasants, priests, and warriors.

Theologians, politicians, and moralists emphasized the cooperation and harmony among these three orders sanctioned by the Trinitarian Godhead. Their complementary functions – supply and maintenance of material life, defense against enemies, and the promotion of spiritual welfare – assisted all in the corpus Christianum to conform to the divine plan. On the other hand, the "divine design" impressed upon the collective consciousness could also sanction social inequalities and exploitation.

The three orders expressed the "feudal" foundation of social relations that lasted in varying degrees up to the French Revolution. The quotation marks indicate that the term "feudal" is a construct by modern historians to describe a social pattern more complicated than the three orders would suggest. Nearly all wealth in the agrarian Middle Ages rested on landholdings and their produce. In feudal society the lord was responsible for protecting his vassals and their lands, and his vassals were obligated to serve the lord through both military service when needed and counsel when called upon. The church was fully involved in the feudal system, having its own fief holdings and lordship as well as being obligated to provide men and material to their lords, secular and religious. The word "lord" was also a term of address to God; and the posture of prayer with hands held together reflected the posture of a vassal doing fealty. By the twelfth century these ideas of lordship and vassalage were also used to describe relationships to women. In courtly literature the man as vassal pledged service to his lady (lord). Hymns to God and the Virgin Mary also began to use this language.

The corpus Christianum encompassed not only such feudal relationships here on earth but also transcended space and time with an ecclesiology that embraced the Christian family in the suffering church in purgatory, the militant church on earth, and the triumphant church in heaven. Through its sacraments the church addressed the major rites of passage in human life from birth to death, and related them to the maintenance of the whole society.

The church's intensive interest in sacraments began very early in its history even though the number of sacraments was not limited to the seven of modern Roman Catholicism (baptism, confirmation, penance, Eucharist, marriage, orders, extreme unction) until the Council of Florence in 1439. The word "sacrament," from the Latin *sacramentum*, translates the Greek term for "mystery." The Latin term originally meant an oath, in particular a soldier's oath of allegiance with its accompanying tattoo of identification. Thus, in the early church, the term itself conveyed the sense that the non-repeatable sacraments – baptism, confirmation, and ordination – impressed an indelible mark, a "tattoo," on the soul.

Baptism initiated a person into the community and the Eucharist nourished the pilgrim traveling toward the heavenly city. The early church had expressed its understanding of the Eucharist in both realistic and symbolic terms. During the Carolingian era, popular piety strengthened and intensified the realistic understanding until it became generally accepted that the bread and wine somehow changed into the body and blood of Christ as the result of priestly consecration of the elements.

There were a number of influences upon this development. The contemporary mentality perceived myriads of miracles and mysteries in nature. It may be that the sacred act of the Eucharist was developed into the wonder of wonders so that it would stand out from the everyday miraculous. Also, the emphasis upon the majesty and omnipotence of God and the growing perception of Christ as divine judge focused attention on the point where the mystery of Christ's presence was most palpable: the Eucharist. Thus the clergy gained social as well as religious power as those who alone could make Christ present in the Eucharist.

A series of eucharistic controversies from the ninth to the eleventh centuries led to the Synod of Rome in 1079, which declared "the bread and wine placed on the altar are, after consecration, not only a sacrament, but also the true body and blood of our Lord Jesus Christ . . . handled by the hands of the priests and crushed by the teeth of the faithful." The doctrine of transubstantiation (Fourth Lateran Council, 1215) later "explained" how this occurred. The sacrament so awed the laity that they began to adore the Host (Latin: *hostia*, a sacrificial victim) and brought their petitions to it. Visions and miracle stories surrounding the sacrament proliferated. Christ as he existed in the sacrament became the greatest of all relics. Popular piety influenced liturgical practices such as a perpetual light before the reserved, consecrated bread; and bells to signal the consecration and elevation of the Host. In 1264 pope Urban IV, influenced by the visions of the French nun Juliana (d. 1258), commanded the Feast of Corpus Christi, the commemoration of the institution of the Eucharist.

The sacrament was so revered that the frequency of reception declined drastically; the sight of the Host alone became a devotional substitute for reception. The laity, fearful of spilling Christ's blood, began withdrawing from taking the cup. In response, the doctrine of concomitance (Council of Constance, 1415) legitimated lay communion with only the bread by affirming the whole Christ in the form of the bread. Since Latin was of little use to the uneducated laity, they no longer "heard" the mass but saw the elevation of the Host as the reenactment of the Passion that the priest, by virtue of the sacrament of orders, "offered" to appease God. By the eve of the Reformation such sacerdotal offerings increased in value as they increased in number.

Nevertheless, the danger of shipwreck on earthly delights was omnipresent. In response to this danger, the church offered the "second plank after shipwreck," the sacrament of penance. The term penance derives from the Latin *poena*, a term that encompasses compensation, satisfaction, expiation, and penalty.

Meditation on the necessity of satisfying the punishment for sin – either here or hereafter – led to the doctrine of purgatory and its purifying fire and the indulgence system for commuting penitential impositions too severe for temporal completion. Thus when cardinal Peter Damian (d. 1072) imposed a 100-year penance on the archbishop of Milan for simony, he also indicated how much money would commute each year of penance. Although the intent of the indulgence system was to adjust satisfaction for sins to changing social conditions, by the late Middle Ages it became so corrupted in service of clerical authority and revenue raising that it evoked Luther's "Ninety-five Theses" on penance and indulgences, sparking the Protestant Reformation.

Individual and collective acts of satisfaction for sin found a variety of outlets. In periods of great social stress, such as the mid-fourteenth-century plague, collective rituals developed such as the penitential bands of flagellants who traveled from town to town scourging themselves. The collective ritual of penance *par excellence* was Lent. Its communal ascetic rigor was such that it spawned a wild collective prelude known as "carnival" (from *carnevalis*, "farewell to flesh") that marked the transition to the meatless period of Lent. Carnival consisted of the days or week preceding Shrove Tuesday, the day before Ash Wednesday, termed in French *Mardi gras*, "fat Tuesday." Carnival was to expose the sins of the community. Carnality, represented as a fat figure carried in procession, was tried, condemned, and executed by fire. The overindulgence in food and drink was vividly expressed by the dedication of Shrove Tuesday in Nantes to St. Dégobillard – St. Vomit! Sexuality and obscenity were equally on display with iconographic representations of the penis such as enormous sausages, as well as symbols of lechery carried in processions that included the town prostitutes. The purpose was to expose that which had been concealed throughout the year, and thus anything regarded as shameful was high on the list for parading.

This was also the period when the hierarchical and patriarchal culture could at least momentarily be overturned, and so men rode backward on asses and women beat the men. The Feast of Fools or the Day of the Boy Bishop, a counterpart to the revels of carnival, often held on January 6, the Feast of Holy Innocents, satirized clerical rules by parading a choirboy as bishop. For a fleeting moment carnival and similar "days of misrule" turned the world upside down.

The Rise of the Mendicant Orders

While not a move to turn the world upside down, the mendicant orders arose from the respective challenges of Dominic (1170–1221) and Francis (ca. 1181–1226) to the socioeconomic and ecclesiastical status quo. The social construction of reality to which the early medieval church had contributed so much now showed signs of stress. The values of stability, tradition, and order expressed in the three orders and the sense of the corpus Christianum set forth by liturgy and ritual were increasingly confronted by change, innovation, and disorder.

The social changes that began around the eleventh century involved population growth and the rise of cities abetted by technological development and a money economy. New personal roles as businessman, citizen, and worker were less all-embracing than the groupings of village and kindred, and involved a shift in relationships and values. An increasing number of people, deprived of kin and community, faced the need to prove themselves rather than play assigned roles. New social experiences exposed them to situations for which the church not only offered no meaningful patterns but also actually resisted changes already underway. What relevance had a religion of stability and humility to a life of mobility and competition? The church's response to these issues tended to reaffirm traditional solutions such as pilgrimage, church building, monastic patronage, eucharistic ritual, and indulgences. The Cluniac and Gregorian renewal movements intended to purify, not change, the church and its theology.

A renewed search for community and divine approbation sought to address the disquieting changes. Both Francis and Dominic incorporated contemporary concerns into their commitment to apostolic poverty as a means for reaching communion with God. In contrast to the Benedictine monasteries that spurned towns as iniquitous, the Franciscans and Dominicans rooted themselves in cities. The Benedictines had emphasized humility, obedience, and stability; poverty to them was understood in terms of poverty of spirit. The mendicant orders, as their name indicates, lived by begging and emphasized material poverty. Their desire to imitate the early church and the wandering, preaching, poor Christ, displaced the older monastic ideal of a fixed role of inter-cession within rural monastic walls with an innovative urban itinerancy; they were able to go to where distressed people longed for the message of the life and poverty of Jesus. For the Benedic-tine monk in his rural cloister, poverty took the form of the denial of self-will and the embrace of humility – achievements correlated with the fact that the Benedictines drew membership from the feudal nobility and warrior class. For the urban mendi-cant monk, poverty was understood in terms of the destitute on the margins of society and the questions of conscience that plagued the new urban entrepreneurs.

Although the Dominicans and Franciscans shared these modern concerns, they differed in their origins and develop-ment. The Dominicans, or Order of Preachers, were founded by the Spanish priest Dominic Guzman. His encounter with an Albigensian innkeeper inspired him to found an order of itinerant preachers. The Albigensians (from Albi, a city in southern France) were a dualistic heretical sect. Also known as Cathars (from the Greek for "pure"), they attracted a wide following due to their ascetic lifestyle and challenge to perceived corruption in the church. After a nightlong effort, Dominic converted the Albigen-sian back to the Catholic faith. The experience made Dominic aware of both the prevalence of the Albigensian heresy and the need for persuasive preaching to counter it. He also realized that only by equaling the ascetic austerity of the heretics would it be possible to preach true doctrine with credibility. Thus voluntary poverty was embraced as a means of promoting an itinerant preaching mission.

In 1216 pope Honorius III recognized Dominic and his followers as an order according to the Rule of St. Augustine, a more flexible rule than the Benedictine Rule. Dominic's concern to counter the doctrinal errors of heretics convinced him of the necessity of a learned ministry. Within Dominic's own lifetime his order became established in the intellectual centers of Paris and Bologna. The intellectual focus of the Dominicans formed such outstanding scholars as Albertus Magnus (ca. 1200–80) and Thomas Aquinas (ca. 1225–74), and led to the papal appointment of the Dominicans as inquisitors in 1232.

The most radical exponent of the new evangelical poverty of the twelfth and thirteenth centuries was Francis of Assisi. Francis lived the ideal of "naked, following the naked Christ" and "poor, following the poor Christ." These twelfth-century formulas, adapted from ancient tradition, associated the individual with Christ in a common nakedness or poverty of worldly goods and cares. Francis vividly embraced this ideal when, nearly 25 years of age, he stood before his angry merchant father and the bishop's court of Assisi and stripped himself naked, gave his clothes to his father, and declared that henceforth he would speak only of his Father in heaven.

For Francis, poverty expressed the imitation of Christ. Francis rejected the new urban merchant world of profits and the accumulation of wealth, the world of his father, as something so corrupt that he regarded money as excrement. He urged his followers to flee money as if it were the devil. The 1223 Rule of St. Francis strictly commanded all friars "never to receive coin or money, for themselves or for any other person." Supposedly, Francis once commanded a friar who had absent-mindedly touched a coin to pick it up with his mouth and to place it in a pile of dung.

Although this attitude would seem unlikely to enhance the recruitment process, it nevertheless worked wonders. Whether Francis touched some deep emotional springs of piety or the nerves and anxieties of the urban, profit-oriented society, his ideal of poverty stimulated a remarkable response from his contemporaries. The enthusiasm for Francis led to the formation of a female branch known as the Poor Clares, after Clare of Assisi, the first woman converted to Francis' ideal of poverty; and then a third order for those unable to embrace the full rigor of Franciscan poverty that permitted remaining in secular life while practicing certain elements of the ideal. Francis soon became the reluctant head of an organization that perceived the whole world as its parish.

Why were Francis and his mendicant order so appealing? Certainly, the medieval person was deeply concerned for personal salvation, the path to which was presented as pilgrimage out of this world. The Franciscans gave the radical ascetic expression of this pilgrimage an orthodox expression. Francis himself reputedly received the stigmata, the very wounds of Christ, the highest expression of medieval piety. But there may well have been other motivations. Rebellion against fathers and the rejection of social respectability were not limited to Francis – or his age! The fact that well-to-do families supported the friars but were horrified by the prospect of their children joining them may have imbued the poverty of the friars with a certain appeal to youth. And for the aspiring intellectuals of the time, the Dominicans and the Franciscans offered a university education without the debts and obligations even then incurred by studies. The desire of scholars to live and work in a university community dovetailed nicely with the needs of friars to educate their new recruits.

The Dominican and Franciscan scholars addressed the social and ethical problems confronting the new urban life. Ironically, they legitimated private property as necessary and good for the development of an ordered state. They developed business ethics and a theory of just price in relation to supply and demand.

These contributions made it possible for the urban Christian merchant, previously marginalized by feudal social mores and a religion that condemned and prohibited usury, to be reintegrated into Christian society. Furthermore, as mendicant orders, the Dominicans and Franciscans provided merchants with a meritorious subject for philanthropy. They provided a key to the justification of profits – how else could one have the wherewithal for charity? – and thus an honorable and much preferred option to the penance and opprobrium that had earlier accrued to businesspersons. The mendicant friars supplied city dwellers with a new ethic and an outlet for charity.

The Dominican and Franciscan vision of the world as their parish and education in preaching as the tool for its conversion, unleashed an intellectual energy that transformed universities from trade schools for training clerks into centers of intellectual ferment and creativity. Such intellectual giants as Albertus Magnus, Thomas Aquinas, and Meister Eckhard (ca. 1260–1327) among the Dominicans, and Bonaventure (ca. 1217–74), Duns Scotus (ca. 1265–1308), and William of Ockham (ca. 1285–1347) among the Franciscans made theology the "queen of the sciences." It is, of course, Aquinas who has long been regarded as one of the most brilliant theologians among the scholastics. The range of his thought and the phenomenal synthesis he achieved in relating reason and revelation imparted such an architectonic and aesthetic quality to his theology that it has been likened to the gothic cathedrals of the time.

Thomas was born into the great feudal family of count Landulf of Aquino that was related to both the emperor and the king of France. In consonance with his family's position and prestige, he was sent as a child to the famous Benedictine monastery of Monte Cassino to be trained to become its abbot. As a teenager, however, Thomas decided to enter the new Dominican order. His father and brothers were furious that Thomas intended to reject the respectable ecclesiastical career customary for the younger sons of nobility for what they and their peers perceived to be an order of ecclesial riffraff. When unable to dissuade Thomas from his decision, the family imprisoned him in the family castle; when that did not work, they decided to render his decision impossible through scandal by putting a courtesan in his room. The story is that young Thomas snatched a brand from the fire, chased the woman from his room, and burned a huge black cross into the door.

Obviously, Thomas' decision was not to be trifled with, and he went on to join the Dominicans studying with Albertus Magnus, who introduced him to the philosophy of Aristotle newly mediated to the West by the Spanish Muslim and Jewish philosophers, Averroes of Cordoba (Ibn Rushd, 1126–98) and Moses Maimonides (1135–1204).

Thomas was and continues to be so influential in the life and thought of the church, not only because he addressed clearly and forcefully the intellectual crisis of the day created by Aristotelian metaphysics that ran counter to revelation, but also because he did so in a way that opened faith to dialogue with philosophy, revelation with empirical reason, religion with science. Thomas slaked his contemporaries' great thirst for reality without giving in to their influential cries that one could drink at only the bar of reason or only the bar of faith but not both. For Thomas, there is only truth, not two mutually exclusive truths. He expressed this conviction in his watchword that grace does not destroy nature but fulfills it; that is, there is continuity between reason and revelation, the natural and the supernatural.

Following Aristotle, Thomas agreed that virtues are acquired through practice and thus become a "habit" – "practice makes perfect." The supernatural virtues, however, unlike the natural virtues, are not innate to humankind but must be infused into the person through God's grace mediated by the church's sacraments. Once infused, the supernatural virtues are, analogously to the natural virtues, to be "acquired" or "realized" by practice. In this sense, the person who is in a state of grace does good works that please God and thus cooperates in his or her salvation. The later scholastic phrase that expresses this process is *facere quod in se est,* "do what is within one." Salvation, then, occurs within one through the actualization of faith formed by acts of charity. The person who does his or her best with the aid of grace receives the reward of eternal life as a just due. Later scholastic theologians would be more optimistic about human capability to cooperate with God in salvation and would suggest that good works done in the state of nature would also be rewarded by God with an infusion of grace as an appropriate due.

Not all of Thomas' contemporaries responded positively to his contributions. The archbishops of Paris and Canterbury condemned several of his propositions in 1277, but in 1278 the General Chapter of the Dominicans endorsed his teaching. He was canonized in 1323 and declared a Doctor of the Church (i.e., official teacher) by pope Pius V (a Dominican) in 1567. In 1879 Leo XIII's encyclical *Aeterni Patris* made Thomas' works mandatory for all students of theology. In 1923, the sixth centenary of his canonization, pope Pius XI reiterated Thomas' teaching authority.

The Rise and Decline of Papal Authority

The age of Thomas was the watershed of the medieval era. It included the ideal Christian monarch (St.) Louis IX of France, the English king Henry III, and Thomas' friend, the great Franciscan theologian and mystic, Bonaventure. The creative synthesis constructed during this period covered all realms of life, including not only reason and revelation, but also sacerdotal authority and personal religious experience. The papal embodiment of the age was Innocent III (r. 1198–1216).

Building upon the centuries-long development of papal ideology, Innocent believed that the whole world is the province of the pope and that Christ had commissioned Peter to govern not only the universal church but also the secular world. A gifted administrator and leader as well as canon lawyer, Innocent expressed his conviction of the superiority of the church over the empire by the analogy that the monarchy is related to the papacy as the moon is to the sun.

Innocent first secured papal power and authority in Rome and then decided a disputed imperial election in favor of Otto IV. However, once secure, Otto IV reneged on his recognition of the papal states and his promise not to intervene in Italy. In response, Innocent appointed Frederick II to replace Otto, and organized a coalition of the papacy, Frederick, and Philip Augustus of France against Otto and his ally, king John of England. This is one of the first great examples of the clash of international alliances in European history. Otto was crushed at the battle of Bouvines in 1214, and Frederick publicly swore an oath of allegiance to the papacy.

Innocent paralleled his triumph in the "imperial business" with the English and French kings. In a dispute concerning traditional royal authority over the English church, Innocent forced king John to accept the papal appointee to the see of Canterbury and to become his vassal, thus making England a fief of the papacy. A sidelight to this was that John acquiesced to Innocent's conditions because in 1213 he was unsure of the support of his barons. When in 1215 the barons rebelled and compelled John to sign the *Magna carta libertatum*, which restricted the crown's feudal and sovereign rights, Innocent supported the king and declared the *Magna carta* null and void.

Innocent also placed France under interdict (cessation of the administration of the sacraments throughout the land) to compel Philip Augustus to be reconciled with his wife, Ingeborg of Denmark. In general, however, Innocent's reign benefited Philip's monarchy. Philip cloaked his expansionist policies in southern France in the dubious morality of a crusade against heretics – the Albigenses whom Dominic had hoped to convert through preaching. When in 1208 a papal legate was murdered in the area, a crusade was launched. Innocent had already been energetically attacking heresy in his own territory and had equated heresy with crime against the sovereign power. Because Innocent did not trust local French officials to purge the remnants of heresy following the bloodbath and land grab of the crusade, he sent papal legates to establish courts to deal with heretics, the basis for the Inquisition.

Although Innocent reorganized the church, humiliated kings, and took up the sword against heretics, he also realized the importance of law and piety for Christendom. He commissioned a collection of canon law, the first since Gratian's *Decretum* (ca. 1140), which became the authentic text for teaching at the University of Bologna. He also recognized the value of the mendicant movements for the renewal and reform of the church, thereby co-opting the claim of heretical movements such as the Albigenses to be the only pure church. Finally, Innocent's summoning of the Fourth Lateran Council in 1215 established one of the most important conciliar meetings since Nicaea in 325. The council set the number of sacraments at the seven still recognized in the Roman Catholic Church; made transubstantiation the orthodox teaching on the Eucharist; limited confirmation and ordination to bishops; mandated at least annual penance and communion for all Catholics; and prohibited the public presence of Jews during Holy Week.

The Decline of the Papacy

With the death of Innocent III the links between hierarchical church authority and the political realm could not be maintained. In little more than a generation after Thomas and Innocent III, king Philip of France subjugated pope Boniface VIII (r. 1294–1303).

Boniface VIII was of Roman noble lineage. He studied law at Bologna and served in the Curia before becoming a cardinal and papal legate to France. An able canon lawyer and administrator,

Boniface represented the legacy of Gregory VII and Innocent III that political facts are subject to papal ideology. Unfortunately for both Boniface and the papal office, the world context had shifted markedly since Innocent's triumphs.

Boniface's troubles began with his feud with the Colonna family, two of whom were cardinals he deposed. Boniface then alienated the kings of England and France, who had moved to tax their clergy to finance their mutual conflict (the Hundred Years' War). In the bull *Clericis laicos* (1296) Boniface forbade clergy to provide ecclesiastical revenue or property to any ruler without consent of the pope and forbade laity to exact or receive taxes from the clergy. The kings were not intimidated. Philip IV of France (1285–1314) responded by banning the export of precious metals, thus cutting off revenue to the papal court.

Boniface caved in and explained that he certainly did not want to invalidate feudal clerical obligations to the crown. Therefore, clergy could provide "voluntary" gifts at the king's "friendly suggestion." In cases of necessity, the king could tax the clergy without papal permission. Finally, to show his "affection" for the French monarchy, Boniface canonized Philip's grandfather, Louis IX.

Unmollified, Philip imprisoned the bishop of Pamiers on various charges. Boniface responded by reinstituting *Clericis laicos*, charging the king with violating the freedom and immunity of the church, and summoning the French bishops to Rome to take measures against the king. Boniface's bull *Ausculta fili* (1301) summoned Philip himself to Rome to answer charges. Undaunted, Philip substituted a forged bull that distorted papal claims along with a proclamation that began: "Your utter fatuity may know that we [the king] are not subjected to anyone." The royal chancery also drew up a list of charges against Boniface that included blasphemy, simony, heresy, fornication, and the murder of the previous pope. At the same time, popular pamphlets and academic treatises attacked Boniface in particular and the papacy in general.

This is the context for one of the most famous and debated decrees of the medieval papacy, *Unam sanctam* (1302), in which Boniface stated that both the temporal and spiritual swords are in the power of the church, that temporal power is subject to the papacy, and that "submission on the part of every man to the bishop of Rome is altogether necessary for his salvation." One of Philip's royal ministers is said to have remarked, "My master's sword is of steel, the pope's is made of verbiage." That point was illustrated by storming the papal palace the night before Boniface was to excommunicate the king. Although liberated by the local populace, Boniface soon died a broken man.

The centuries-long development of the ideal of a universal Christian commonwealth with one emperor, one language, and one law under the church, the ark of salvation captained by the papacy, ran aground on the rocks thrust up with the development of national vernaculars, states, and laws. Since the Donation of Constantine, papal ideology had focused attention on the empire and the emperor, and had neglected those rulers whom Gregory VII referred to as mere "kinglets." But these kinglets had become aware of a new national sense and outlook for which the papacy had little or no ideological means of control. Philip's triumph over Boniface concluded one phase in the history of the papacy and initiated another.

Conciliarism

Traumatized by the attack upon Boniface, the papacy attempted to appease France and to restore its own prestige. However, matters only deteriorated with the election of the archbishop of Bordeaux as Clement V (r. 1305–14). He ensconced the papacy in Avignon, a city under the influence of France. Thus began what the Italian poet Francesco Petrarch (1304–74) termed the "Babylonian captivity" of the church (1309–77), during which all the popes were French. A French pope with a French Curia lived in a French-speaking city on the French frontier. The papacy, that under Innocent III had subdued kings and emperors, was now widely perceived to be captive to the French monarchy.

Critical voices were increasingly raised against the papacy. The French Dominican John of Paris (ca. 1250–1306) argued in his *On Papal and Royal Power* that secular government was rooted in the natural human community and that popes had no power therefore to depose kings. Marsilius of Padua (ca. 1275–1342), a former rector of the University of Paris, in *The Defender of the Peace* (1324) blamed the papacy for undermining world peace. His solution was to limit the authority of the papacy by the laws governing all human institutions, laws that derived from the whole community based on Aristotle and Roman law. Dante (1265–1321) assailed the papacy and popes not only in his *Divine Comedy* but also in his *On Monarchy*. In the latter he argued the papacy should abandon all temporal authority and possessions, and that temporal peace required a universal monarchy under the emperor. Petrarch, who had lived in and around Avignon for some years, described the luxury and worldliness of the papal court and building program there as "the sewer of the world." Instead of responding to the philosophical, theological, and literary critiques, the papacy concentrated on bureaucratic efficiency for collecting more and more money, shuffling its thousands of pages of documents concerned with benefices, indulgences, politics, and patronage.

With papal prestige at a low point, there were increasing calls for the papacy to return to Rome, including pressure by the influential women mystics Catherine of Siena (d. 1380) and Bridget of Sweden (d. 1373). Finally, the papacy in the person of Gregory XI (r. 1370–8) reentered Rome and took up official residency at the Vatican. Ironically, this move led almost immediately to the Western Schism of the church.

Conflict over Gregory's successor led to the election of a rival pope. There had been antipopes before in the history of the church, but this was the first time that the same College of

Cardinals had legitimately elected two popes. Urban VI, successor to Gregory, refused to accede to the cardinals' request that he abdicate. He and his successors remained in Rome. Clement VII, elected to replace Urban, and his successors returned to Avignon. It is difficult today to appreciate the depth of the religious insecurity and the intensity of institutional criticism caused by this schism. If, as decreed by *Unam sanctam*, salvation itself was contingent on obedience to the pope, it was crucial to know who was the true Vicar of Christ. But how could this be decided?

Europe itself was split. France, Scotland, Aragon, Castille, and Navarre followed the Avignon line; whereas much of Germany, Hungary, England, Poland, and Scandinavia followed the Roman line. Public opinion was hopelessly confused. Even the learned and the holy clashed over who was the true pope. Catherine of Siena promoted universal recognition of Urban. She called the cardinals who elected Clement "fools, liars, and devils in human form." On the other hand, the Spanish Dominican Vincent Ferrar was equally zealous for the Avignon popes, and labeled the adherents of Urban "dupes of the devil and heretics." The maintenance of two papal courts and their related expenses increased the ecclesial tax burdens; and the disputing popes' appointments of partisans to bishoprics and ecclesial benefices furthered division and acrimony.

The first attempt to resolve the crisis by an ecumenical council, proposed by various professors and universities, occurred with the Council of Pisa (1409). Both popes refused to attend, and thus the council deposed both and elected a new pope, Alexander V (r. 1409–10), a cardinal of the Roman line. The deposed popes, however, declined to recognize the validity of the council, and thus there were now three popes!

To make a long and complicated story blessedly short, the emperor Sigismund, in line with the precedent set by Constantine, accepted arguments that a general council is superior to the pope and that as emperor and protector of the church he had the duty to call a council. He convoked the Council of Constance

(1414–18) to deal with three main issues: the great schism, reform of the church in "head and members," and the extirpation of heresy. In the matter of heresy, the council condemned to death the Englishman John Wyclif (ca. 1330–84) and the Czech Jan Hus (ca. 1372–1415) for heresy. Wyclif cheated the verdict by already being dead, but the burning of Hus, who had been given a safe conduct to come to the council, ignited religious fires in Bohemia that were still burning by the time of the Reformation a century later.

The major agenda item, however, had to do with the schism. The council decided to vote by nations rather than by individuals, with each nation having one vote. The decision counterbalanced the preponderance of Italian prelates upon whom the Roman pope was depending. It was also a democratizing decision because it gave voice to non-prelates. Furthermore, the idea of a nation as a unit contributed to the already developing sense of nationalism that was undermining the old idea of a universal Christian commonwealth under the headship of the papacy.

The council successfully resolved the schism with the election of Martin V. In the process the council passed two significant decrees, *Haec sancta* and *Frequens*. The former placed the authority of an ecumenical council over that of a pope in matters of faith and reform of the church. The latter decreed frequent and regular meetings of ecumenical councils "in perpetuity." Martin V did not confirm or approve the council, an omission probably little noted in the midst of the profound relief at having resolved the schism. His successor, Eugene IV (r. 1431–47), approved the Council of Constance insofar as it was not prejudicial to the rights and supremacy of the papacy. And Pius II (r. 1458–64) in his bull *Execrabilis* (1460) prohibited any and all appeals to a council over the pope; such an appeal in itself to be regarded as heresy and schism.

Further councils – Basel (1433), Ferrara-Florence (1439) – did not accomplish much other than to affirm the view of Pius II and other one-time conciliarists that parliamentary government was not to their liking. Rulers sensed that conciliarism implied too large a voice for the governed. With the demotion of the papacy to the status of one monarchical government among others, it dawned on monarchs that conciliarism was a two-edged sword – the means called upon to control the papacy might become a weapon against them. Consequently, the papacy and monarchs became disposed to cooperate and to conclude concordats with each other for the sake of mutual support. The papacy's efforts to overcome the challenge of conciliarism and to consolidate its patrimony in Italy diverted its energy and attention from the widespread cry for reform of the church in head and members.

In less than a century this cry would become the full-throated roar of the Reformation that blew away the last vestiges of the ideal of the corpus Christianum. Although that roar would include a cacophony of voices, its first sighs and murmurs came from those alienated by poverty, the profit economy, and the stress of urban growth augmented by fears of famine, plague, and war, the anger of the frustrated renewal movements of Wyclif and Hus, and the individualism and intellectual discoveries of the Renaissance.

Chapter 8

The Reformations of the Sixteenth Century

The Reformation era is customarily dated from 1517 and the posting of Martin Luther's "Ninety-five Theses," to 1555 and the Religious Peace of Augsburg. In this short period the Roman papal hegemony over Western Christendom was shattered, and Catholicism came to be known as "Roman Catholicism," now one denomination of Christianity among others. Four major churches arose in this period – Roman Catholic, Lutheran, Reformed (the general name for the various national Calvinist churches), and Anglican – with a variety of other Christian communities – Anabaptists and Spiritualists – espousing more radical reforms. The late-Reformation polarization of Christendom into conflicting denominations with specific confessions of faith is known as the "confessional period." The confessional period extended to the Peace of Westphalia (1648) that concluded the Thirty Years' War (1618–48), the last of the major religious wars stemming from the Reformation.

Context

On the eve of the Reformation the question was not whether the church *should* be reformed but *when*. The papacy, earlier buffeted by conciliarism and national renewal movements, now faced the challenges of the intellectual awakening known as the Renaissance. The watchword of the Renaissance that began in fourteenth-century Italy and spread northward was *ad fontes* – "back to the sources" – of Western culture: the Greek and Latin classics, the Bible, and the writings of the church fathers. Scholars such as Desiderius Erasmus (1469–1536) and Jacques Lefèvre d'Etaples (ca. 1460–1536) provided editions of the New Testament and biblical prefaces and commentaries that went behind the Latin Vulgate to the Greek text, and thereby stimulated a critical rereading of the theological tradition. Other texts too came under the sharp eye and literary methods of the humanists; for example, Lorenzo Valla (ca. 1406–57) proved that the famous Donation of Constantine was spurious. New ideas spread rapidly, widely, and reliably due to the recent invention of the printing press, and found homes in new universities such as the University of Wittenberg, founded in 1502. Indeed, Luther wrote to a friend that courses on the Bible and Augustine's writings were displacing the study of Aristotelian metaphysics and ethics and scholastic theology at Wittenberg. In a sense, then, the Reformation began in a faculty-led curriculum change – hard to believe if you've ever had to sit through a faculty meeting!

Stimulated by the recovery of biblical and early church texts and the excitement of fresh translations and interpretations, reformers throughout Europe urged biblical preaching and pastoral theology. Preachers became translators and translators became preachers. Their conviction that academic theology serves the proclamation of the gospel was succinctly expressed in Erasmus' rendering of the opening verses of the Gospel of John: "In the beginning was the *sermon*." But at the very time the reformers were bringing theology out of the scholastic closet with vernacular sermons and devotional writings, the papacy had reached an advanced stage in the hardening of its pastoral and ethical arteries.

A series of worldly popes not only bequeathed glorious art and architecture to posterity but also anger and anxiety to their contemporaries. Stung by the conciliar movement's encroachment upon papal authority, the major figures of the late medieval papacy sought to squelch voices of renewal. Their success in containing conciliarism may be seen in that, apart from the Council of Trent (1545–63), the late and grudging response to the Reformation, there was not another council until Vatican I (1869–70), which in its declaration of papal primacy and infallibility definitively answered the Council of Constance.

Contemporaries experienced cognitive dissonance when they perceived the opulence and power of the papal court in contrast to the biblical image of the shepherd guarding his flock. Critics pointed out that Jesus' command to Peter was "feed my sheep" (John 21:15–17), not "fleece them." A German woodcut portrayed the mercenary spirit of the papacy by picturing the pope and the Curia counting money in one panel and Jesus driving the moneychangers from the temple in the opposite panel. An Italian proverb stated that the person who goes to Rome will lose his or her faith. And a Latin acrostic for Rome summed up the sense of papal venality: *R[adix] O[mnium] M[alorum] A[varitia]* – "the love of money is the root of all evil." The papacy had become a regal court, and the pope was increasingly perceived to be nothing more than an Italian prince. Two particularly notorious popes exemplify this papal image: Alexander VI (r. 1492–1503) and Julius II (r. 1503–13).

Rodrigo Borgia was made a cardinal by his uncle, pope Callistus III, and won the papacy largely through bribery, taking the title Alexander VI. It is no surprise that continuing familial and financial concerns determined Alexander's reign, rooted in nepotism and simony from the beginning. He is one pope to whom the title "father," if not "holy," may be literally applied. Alexander's involvement in sexual promiscuity, alleged poisonings, and murderous intrigues made the name Borgia a synonym for corruption. He was denounced in his own time by the influential and fiery Dominican preacher Girolamo Savonarola (1452–98), who, unmoved by bribes or threats, was executed in Florence. Alexander's efforts to strengthen the papacy abetted French intervention in northern Italy that in turn contributed to a new period of power politics with Italy as the focus of international intrigue.

Julius II, like Alexander a patron of the arts, supported Raphael, Michelangelo, and Bramante. Julius' enthusiasm for rebuilding St. Peter's – the goal of which was to show other princes that the pope had a more magnificent court – was matched by his zeal for war. So much of his reign involved warfare that people began to wonder what this pontiff had to do with the Prince of Peace. Erasmus, who witnessed Julius' triumphal martial entry into Bologna, satirized him in *Julius Excluded* by depicting him in full armor trying unsuccessfully to force his way into heaven.

Julius' successor was a son of the famous Florentine banking family, the Medici. He took the title Leo X (r. 1513–21). He revealed his sensitivity to the widespread desire for reform of the church by reputedly opening his reign with the words: "Now that God has given us the papacy, let us enjoy it." But as Leo was settling into the papal throne, a young monk named Martin Luther (1483–1546) was struggling to understand the Bible in a newly established university in the German backwater town of Wittenberg.

Luther's reform movement was not initiated by the moral indignation of a Savonarola directed against the Renaissance papacy, but by his anxiety about salvation. Luther and fellow reformers were confronted by this in the praxis of the worshipping community. Hence it is important to remember that Luther's formal academic disputation "Disputation on the Power and Efficacy of Indulgences," better known as the "Ninety-five Theses," focused on the sacrament of penance and its associated issues of justification, indulgences, purgatory, and ecclesiastical authority. In brief, the Reformation began with a focus on the central pastoral praxis of the church: the forgiveness of sins.

The Reformation in Germany

The personal and pastoral problem that plagued Luther was whether salvation is achieved or received. The medieval scholastic answer that it is both did not resolve the issue for him because the necessity of even the smallest human contribution to salvation threw the burden of proof back upon the person. The church's pastoral care made people uncertain of their salvation and thus more dependent upon the intercessions of the church by stimulating spiritual anxiety and introspection in stressing that "no one knows whether he is worthy of God's love or hate" (Ecclesiastes 9:1). Furthermore, people did not need to go to confession to feel insecure and uncertain about their salvation. Everywhere in everyday life, images – those "books of the laity" in pope Gregory the Great's phrase – served to remind people of heaven and hell. Medieval churches presented the image of Christ on the throne of judgment with a sword and a lily extending from either side of his head. The lily represents resurrection to heaven, but the sword of judgment to eternal torment was more vivid in the minds of most people. Pictures and poems presented the theme of the "dance of death" complete with a skeletal Grim Reaper, and provided manuals on the "art of dying."

Luther's teaching responsibilities at Wittenberg as well as his own quest for certainty of salvation led him to intensive study of the Bible. Here he discovered that righteousness before God is not what the sinner achieves but what the sinner receives as a free gift from God. The promise that salvation is no longer the goal of life but rather the foundation of life freed him from preoccupation with his own spiritual pulse and for life in the world. Luther reversed the medieval piety of achievement: good works do not make the sinner acceptable to God, but rather God's acceptance of the sinner prompts good works.

Luther's personal discovery became a public event with his criticism of current indulgence practices in the "Ninety-five Theses." The popular mind, abetted by some preachers, had twisted the meaning of indulgence from that of the remission of a church-imposed penance after priestly absolution to that of a ticket to heaven. Hard-sell medieval indulgence sellers such as John Tetzel offered direct access to heaven even for the dead in purgatory. One of Tetzel's sales jingles was: "As soon as the coin into the box rings, a soul from purgatory to heaven springs." Tetzel's extravagant claims for the power of an indulgence included remission of sin even if one had raped the Virgin Mary. Another claim, according to popular lore, ricocheted back upon Tetzel to his own dismay. A knight bought an indulgence on the basis that it extended to future sins and then robbed Tetzel!

Aside from such an occasional glitch, Tetzel was a well-paid, excellent salesman who today would be the envy of the advertising world. He entered towns with fanfares of trumpets and drums and the flags and symbols of the papacy. Quite a show in the pre-television age! After a vivid sermon on hell in the town square, he proceeded to the largest church and gave an equally vivid sermon on purgatory and the sufferings awaiting the audience and presently endured by their dear departed friends and relatives. After the next sermon depicting heaven, his audience was sufficiently prepped and eager to buy indulgences.

Luther's theses directed at Tetzel's abuse of indulgences were written in Latin, and most Wittenbergers could not even read German. Thus the popular image of Luther as the angry young man pounding incendiary theses to a church door is more romantic fiction than reality. The uproar originated from the fact that Luther sent the theses to Tetzel's superior, archbishop Albrecht of Mainz, with the naive thought that Albrecht did not know his hireling was abusing the authority of the church. In actuality, Luther had unknowingly touched the nerve of a far-reaching political and ecclesiastical scam. Pope Leo X needed funds to build St. Peter's, and Albrecht had agreed to provide such funds in return for a papal dispensation to become the archbishop of Mainz.

Events accelerated rapidly as the establishment proceeded to silence Luther. By January 1521 Luther was excommunicated, and the papacy urged the young, newly elected emperor, Charles V, to issue a mandate against Luther. But the German constitution and Charles' coronation oath upheld the right of Germans to a trial by impartial judges. Thus Luther was promised safe conduct to a hearing at the impending Diet of Worms in April. There, before the emperor, princes, lords, and ecclesiastical authorities – a world away from his monastic cell and classroom – Luther did not receive a hearing but was presented with a pile of his writings and asked to recant their errors. His brief answer that he could not go against his conscience unless convinced by scripture or clear reason included the memorable phrase, "Here I stand, may God help me." The result, the Edict of Worms (1521), proclaimed Luther an outlaw to be seized and delivered to the authorities. Fortunately for Luther, he had a number of powerful supporters, including his own prince, Frederick the Wise, who sequestered Luther in one of his castles for safekeeping. During the six months of Luther's "castle arrest" he translated the New Testament into German.

The Reformation motif of faith active in love energized innovative approaches to a broad range of early modern social issues including reform of social welfare, literacy and public education, and political issues of authority and the right to resistance. The Reformers' rejection of mandatory clerical celibacy not only struck at church authority but "civil"-ized the clergy in the sense that they became citizens with homes, families, and a stake in civil responsibilities. The liberation from striving for salvation released human energy and material resources for this-worldly activities.

While Luther referred to the early evangelical movement in Wittenberg as "our theology," fissures among erstwhile colleagues began appearing by the early 1520s. Andreas Bodenstein von Karlstadt (1486–1541), sometimes referred to as the forerunner of Puritanism, insisted that evangelical insights must be instituted without tarrying for anyone. One effect of this, paralleled in other centers of reform such as Zurich, was an outbreak of iconoclasm during efforts to sweep out the old faith. Luther's response was that to coerce people into gospel perspectives by forced reform was only to revert back to a religion of laws, and thus undermines the insight that justification is a free gift.

Tensions and conflicts between the German Reformers escalated in relation to the Peasants' War (1524–5) as Thomas Müntzer (ca. 1490–1525) joined the late phase of the war with the rallying cry that "the godless have no right to live." The extremely volatile mix of late medieval apocalypticism and oppressive social and economic conditions coupled with the Reformation motifs of the "freedom of the Christian" and theological critiques of canon law and papal authority, fueled the peasants' social and religious expectations for political and economic liberation, but horribly misfired at their disastrous defeat at Frankenhausen in 1525.

The emperor Charles V's (1500–58) military preoccupations with France (the Habsburg–Valois Wars, 1521–59) and the Ottoman Empire (Sultan Süleyman I the Magnificent, r. 1520–66) continually frustrated his efforts to eliminate the Reformation movements in his realm apart from his hereditary lands, the Low Countries. Charles also needed the support of the Protestant princes in his military campaigns. The Protestant princes presented a confession of their faith to the emperor at the 1530 Diet of Augsburg. Composed by Luther's colleague, Philip Melanchthon (1497–1560), the Augsburg Confession did not sway the Catholic emperor to rescind the Edict of Worms, but it did become the foundational document for Lutheran churches up to today.

The rejection of the Augsburg Confession led the Protestants to form a military alliance, the Schmalkald League, that protected the Protestant movement until its defeat by imperial forces in 1547. By this time, however, the evangelicals had gained sufficient strength that a series of settlements led finally to their toleration in the 1555 Peace of Augsburg, with the principle that the religion of the ruler would be the religion of the territory (*cuius regio, eius religio*, "whose reign, his religion").

The Reformation in Switzerland

The Reform movement in Switzerland proceeded along roughly parallel lines in Zurich under the leadership of Huldrych Zwingli (1484–1531), and then in Geneva under the leadership of John Calvin (1509–64). Unlike Luther, these Reformers lacked the protection of a benevolent and supportive prince and thus had to develop and implement their movements in cooperation (and tension) with their respective civic governments.

Zwingli's renown for biblical study and preaching led to his 1518 appointment by the city government to the major preaching post in Zurich. His commitment to the Reformation principle *sola scriptura* was evident immediately. His sermons, no longer based upon the church's lectionary, methodically exposited book after biblical book. By 1525 he had established "prophesyings," weekly Bible studies for the Zurich clergy and advanced students. A similar practice was established in Geneva in 1536 under Calvin. All of life, personal and communal, was to be normed by scripture.

Controversy, however, soon erupted on multiple fronts. At home, Zwingli and his colleagues found themselves in a double-fronted conflict with those who wanted to halt reforms and those who wanted to expand and radicalize them. Hugo, the bishop of Constance, whose diocese included Zurich, led the former; Conrad Grebel (1498–1526), the reputed founder of Anabaptism, led the latter. The Anabaptists (i.e., "re-baptists"), in applying biblical norms to faith and life, understood baptism to be contingent upon a mature confession of faith rather than a sacrament administered to infants who neither understood nor evidenced a Christian life. The Anabaptist confession of faith, the Schleitheim Confession (1527), also rejected what most of their contemporaries assumed were normal obligations of citizenship: oaths, tithes, and military service.

Added to these challenges facing Zwingli was the years-long dispute with Luther over the correct interpretation of the Lord's Supper. The German Lutheran prince Philip of Hesse, hoping for a united Protestant front against Catholic military forces, brought Luther and Zwingli to the negotiating table in Marburg in 1529. At the Marburg Colloquy the Lutherans and Zwinglians agreed on 14 of 15 articles. They repudiated transubstantiation and the belief that the mass is a sacrifice for the living and the dead, and they insisted upon communion in both kinds. However, the two evangelical parties remained apart on whether the Lord's Supper is primarily an act of thanksgiving for the gospel (Zwingli's symbolic and memorial view) or a concrete offer of the gospel (Luther's sacramental emphasis on Christ's real presence). The differing Protestant theologies of the Eucharist continued to be church dividing in spite of Calvin's later ecumenical efforts informed by his own emphasis upon the gift character of the sacrament. Calvin did achieve agreement with Zwingli's successor, Heinrich Bullinger (1504–75) with the Consensus Tigurinus (1549), but by this time many second generation Lutherans suspected this was more Zwinglian than Lutheran.

Unable to achieve recognition at the Diet of Augsburg in 1530, Zurich was vulnerable to Swiss Catholic pressures. In 1531 the Zurich forces were routed at the Second Battle of Kappel, during which Zwingli was killed. The consequent political resolution that divided Switzerland by confessional allegiance foreshadowed the fate of Europe.

At the time of Zwingli's death, Geneva had not yet adopted the Reformation and neither had its future Reformer-to-be, John Calvin, who was just completing his legal studies in France. Sometime in 1533–4 Calvin experienced his so-called "unexpected conversion." Trained in law and imbued with humanist learning, Calvin echoed Luther's fundamental understanding of salvation. In his *Institutes of the Christian Religion* Calvin described justification by faith in terms of God's acquittal of the guilty sinner.

In early 1535 Calvin sought refuge in Basel from the intensifying persecution of Protestants in his native France. Here he completed and published the first edition of his *Institutes* prefaced by a masterful appeal to king Francis I for a fair hearing of the evangelical faith. Calvin then concluded his affairs in France and set out for the city of Strasbourg where he hoped to settle down to a life of evangelical scholarship. Forced to detour through Geneva, Calvin was confronted by his compatriot, Guillaume Farel (1489–1565), who had been preaching reform in Geneva since 1532. Only months before Calvin's arrival in July 1536, Geneva had finally achieved independence, with the aid of its neighbor Bern, from the Duchy of Savoy and its imposed episcopal rule. The citizens voted to adopt the Reformation and to expel all clergy who disagreed. Farel, faced by the enormous task of institutionalizing reform in Geneva, made it clear in no uncertain terms to Calvin that God had sent Calvin to Geneva for precisely this task. Furthermore, Calvin was told that to shirk this duty would incur his damnation; Calvin stayed!

The reforming colleagues' emphasis upon church discipline soon alienated the Geneva council and many of its citizens. Exiled in 1538, Calvin now finally made it to Strasbourg where he spent the next years learning about institutional reform and church organization from that city's reformer, Martin Bucer (1491–1551). Here, too, he married. Geneva, now concerned about faltering reform, appealed to Calvin to return. Not without misgivings, but with the promise that he could develop a reformed order for the church, Calvin returned in 1541. Within six weeks of his return Calvin completed and submitted to the magistrates of Geneva his *Ecclesiastical Ordinances*. Soon ratified, the *Ordinances* organized the Genevan church according to four categories of ministry: doctors, pastors, deacons, and elders. The doctors were to maintain doctrinal purity through theological study and instruction. Pastors were responsible for preaching, administering the sacraments, and admonishing the people. Deacons were responsible for the supervision of poor relief and the hospitals. Elders were responsible for maintaining discipline within the community. The institutional organ for church discipline was the Consistory, a kind of ecclesiastical court, including the pastors and elders. The Consistory was a bone of contention through most of Calvin's career in Geneva due to its supervision of public morality and its power to excommunicate.

Challenges to Calvin's authority came not just from those who resented what they considered meddling by the Consistory. Two doctrinal debates threatened to unravel the fabric of "the most perfect school of Christ," as the Scottish reformer John Knox (1513–72) called Geneva. The first was a sharp public attack on Calvin's doctrine of predestination by Jerome Bolsec (ca. 1524–84), who claimed it was unbiblical. The charge that the Genevan reformers were unclear about a point of scripture was not a narrow theological challenge because the reform movement rested upon popular confidence in its biblical basis. Calvin's response was to reiterate that predestination is an expression of unconditional grace – God chooses the sinner, not vice versa. Bolsec himself was banished from Geneva.

The second controversy was the trial and execution of Michael Servetus (ca. 1511–53) for his denial of the doctrine of the Trinity. Already notorious throughout Europe for his written attacks on the Trinity, Servetus escaped execution in France (where the Catholics had to be satisfied with burning him in effigy) and ended up in Geneva where the Protestants did the "honor." From a political perspective, the Genevans were in a bind if they did not try and execute Servetus because the city had gained a reputation as the haven for heretics, but the operative motive was theological. It was this to which the Genevan schoolmaster exiled by Calvin, Sebastian Castellio (1515–63), responded when he wrote: "To burn a heretic is not to defend a doctrine but to kill a person." Castellio's *Concerning Heretics, Whether They are to be Persecuted* is one of the best known early modern pleas for religious toleration.

Calvin's Protestant contemporaries did not view Geneva as a vengeful theocracy. Thousands of religious refugees flocked to Geneva from nearly every province in France, as well as from England, Scotland, Holland, Italy, Spain, Germany, Poland, and Bohemia. When they returned home, they took Calvinism with them.

The Reformation in France

Once Calvin's leadership was established in Geneva, he and the French exiles living there directed an effective evangelization program toward France. Although French Calvinists were called Huguenots, they preferred the term Reformed. By 1567 over a hundred pastors sent from Geneva were organizing Reformed congregations patterned on the Geneva church. In 1559 the first national synod of the Reformed church in France met in Paris. Calvin himself provided the first draft of its confession of faith, the Gallican Confession. It was modified at the Synod of La Rochelle in 1571 and continues to inform French Reformed churches to this day.

The crown played a major role in the course of the Reformation in France. Until the late 1520s, reform-minded humanists and reformers found shelter under Francis I's enthusiasm for Renaissance humanism. But the Gallican tradition of "one king, one law, one faith" plus the crown's considerable power over the church guaranteed by the Concordat of Bologna (1516) precluded state endorsement of Reformation ideas. By 1516 Francis I had everything that the English king Henry VIII broke with the church to get. Thus, as Reformation ideas began to take root not only in the "middle class" but also in the nobles of the Bourbon (next in line for the throne after the ruling Valois) and Mont-morency houses, the crown began a policy of persecution to root out Protestantism.

The resulting civil strife prompted the crown's call for a public Protestant–Catholic debate. Any hope that the Colloquy of Poissy (1561) would contribute to peace was dashed when Theodore Beza (1519–1605), Calvin's heir apparent in Geneva and leader of the Huguenot delegation, unequivocally rejected the bodily presence of Christ in the sacrament. To Beza and his colleagues, the Catholic belief that the mass was the community's supreme good work of offering and receiving the corporeal Christ was no more than idolatry and rejection of the gospel. The Catholic rage against such blasphemy was not merely a reaction to theological disputation, but reflected the offenses visited upon their faith by a generation of iconoclasts who had desecrated churches and holy objects, including the consecrated sacramental bread.

The crown's effort to overcome the failure at Poissy by an Edict of Toleration (January 1562) lasted barely two months before armed attacks on Huguenot congregations occurred, and the country sank into decades of conflict fueled by religious hatred. The most infamous event in the French Wars of Religion was the St. Bartholomew's Day Massacre (August 24, 1572), when thousands of Huguenots were massacred in a frenzy of state terrorism. A generation later, weary of bloodshed and assassinations, the Protestant Bourbon, Henry of Navarre, became king as Henry IV, converted to Catholicism ("Paris is worth a mass"), and set forth a policy of limited toleration in the Edict of Nantes (1598) that lasted until its revocation by Louis XIV in 1685.

The Reformation in England

The traditional view of the English Reformation as an act of state reflects Henry VIII's (1491–1547; reigned from 1509) break with Rome over his desire for a divorce. Indeed, the top-down imposition of ecclesiology continued in his heirs: Protestantism with Edward VI (1537–53); Catholicism with Mary Tudor (1516–58); and Protestantism with Elizabeth I (1533–1603). Yet, without gainsaying the significant roles of the various Tudors, the Reformation in England benefited from a residual Lollard anticlericalism, humanist interest in reform, and continental Reformation influences spread by young Cambridge scholars, pamphlets, Bible translations, the return of English students studying in the centers of Switzerland, and then the influx of Protestant refugees from continental Europe. Later, with the accession of Elizabeth I (1558), the Marian exiles returned from such Protestant centers as Frankfurt and Geneva and began to radicalize reforms in England in the direction of Puritanism.

English translations of the Bible were significant means of introducing Reformation ideas. William Tyndale (ca. 1494–1536), one of the most influential translators, carried out most of his work in exile on the Continent. His translation of the New Testament (first printed in 1525) utilized Luther's translation and included many of Luther's biblical prefaces. Miles Coverdale (1488–1568) assisted Tyndale in translating the Old Testament, and was responsible for the first complete English translation of the Bible (1535). Largely through the influence of Thomas Cromwell (ca. 1485–1540), Henry VIII's chief minister in state and church, and archbishop Thomas Cranmer (1489–1556), the king was persuaded to put the Bible in all the churches.

Theological ideas were not however the source for the English break with Rome, but rather the king's "great matter." Henry's marriage to his brother's widow, Catherine of Aragon, arranged for an alliance with Spain, necessitated a papal dispensation because Leviticus 18:6–18 prohibited marriages within close relationships. The only child to survive from the marriage was Mary Tudor. Henry wanted a male heir and hoped Anne Boleyn would do the honors. He appealed to pope Clement VII for an annulment on the biblical basis that one should not marry a brother's widow (Leviticus 20:21). Henry's demand put Clement in an ecclesiastical and political bind. If he granted an annulment he would undermine papal authority by reversing a previous pope's action. The political problem was that Clement was virtually a prisoner of the emperor Charles V (the Sack of Rome, 1527), who as Catherine's nephew was adamantly opposed to Henry's plan to divorce her. Henry's solution, after a long and convoluted process, was to get satisfaction through the English courts. To free himself from papal interference, Henry declared himself and his successors head of the Church of England (Act of Supremacy, 1534). Henry wanted Rome out of his realm, but not Catholicism. Hence the Act of Six Articles (1539) reaffirmed pre-Reformation orthodoxy.

Reformation theology – oriented to the Swiss Reformed – came to the fore during the reign of the child king, Edward VI (1547–53). Cranmer provided the Prayer Book (1549, revised 1552) and a statement of faith, the Forty-two Articles (revised to Thirty-nine Articles under Elizabeth). The tide was reversed with the accession of the ardent Roman Catholic Mary to the throne (1553–8). Ironically, her efforts to restore Catholicism strengthened Protestant resolve. Her marriage to Philip of Spain linked her faith to foreign influence; her efforts to restore church properties alienated their present owners; her persecution of Protestants created the host of martyrs celebrated by John Foxe's (1517–87) martyrology; and through the flight of hundreds of leading Protestants she exposed English Protestants to continental theology that they eagerly brought back upon her death.

The pendulum of reform swung to the middle with Elizabeth, whose long reign (1558–1603) facilitated the establishment of English Protestantism. Elizabeth's *via media* retained traditional vestments and an English liturgy with sermons and prayers normed by the Thirty-nine Articles. The theology of the Eucharist, perennial focal point of dispute, denied transubstantiation on the one hand and Zwinglian symbolism on the other, while remaining open to a range of Lutheran and Calvinist interpretations. As

"Supreme Governor" of the church (1559 Act of Supremacy), Elizabeth proceeded to appoint moderate clergy who conformed to her program. Significant support came from such apologists as John Jewel (1522–71; *Apology for the Anglican Church*) and Richard Hooker (ca. 1554–1600; *Treatise on the Laws of Ecclesiastical Polity*). Elizabeth responded to Catholic challenges by executing her Catholic rival, Mary Stuart, Queen of Scots (1587), and destroying the Spanish Armada (1588). The challenge from Calvinists of varying persuasions was a continual bother, with "Presbyterians" rejecting episcopal polity and "Puritans" striving to purify the church of all vestiges of Catholicism. Elizabeth charted a course between Catholicism and Calvinism because the former denied her legitimacy and the latter rejected the episcopacy she believed supported monarchy. In order to rule the Church of England through her bishops, she had to reject the decentralized polity of European Reformed churches and of Scottish Presbyterianism. Her successor, James I, agreed with his succinct phrase: "No bishop, no king."

Scandinavia and Eastern Europe

Humanism and Catholic reform movements prepared the ground for the introduction of the Reformation in Denmark, that then included Norway, Iceland, a number of provinces in present-day Sweden, and the associated duchies of Schleswig and Holstein where the Danish king was duke. Lutheran influences were evident in Schleswig already in the early 1520s, and king Christian III (r. 1534–59) officially established the Lutheran Reformation in Denmark in 1537. The king's own evangelical commitment may have begun when he saw Luther at the Diet of Worms; he later married a Lutheran, corresponded extensively with Luther, Melanchthon, and Bugenhagen on theological subjects, and provided economic support to the Wittenberg reformers. Christian appointed Luther's colleague, Johannes Bugenhagen

(1485–1558), known as the "Reformer of the North" for his introduction of the Wittenberg reforms throughout northern German cities and his native Pomerania, to lead the reform of the Danish church. Stationed in Copenhagen from 1537 to 1539, Bugenhagen led the reorganization of the church, ordaining seven Lutheran bishops, thus ending apostolic succession, and reforming the University of Copenhagen according to the model of the University of Wittenberg. Influential Danish theologians such as the bishops Peder Palladius, Hans Tausen, and Niels Palladius were trained at Wittenberg. In 1538 the Augsburg Confession was made the foundational document of the Danish church.

Olaus Petri and his brother Laurentius, previously students in Wittenberg, brought Luther's theology to Sweden-Finland. The Swedish king Gustavus Vasa (r. 1523–60) established the Reformation there in 1527. One consequence in Finland was the sending of Finnish students to Wittenberg, the most famous being Michael Agricola (ca. 1510–57). Agricola is known as the father of written Finnish through his prayer book (1544) and New Testament translation (1548). In Eastern Europe the Reformation was established in Prussia and Livonia but remained a minority movement in other areas.

Early Modern Catholicism

Well before Luther came on the scene, Catholic renewal found personal expression in such movements as the Beguines and Beghards (twelfth century), the Brethren of the Common Life or Devotio Moderna (late fourteenth century), and institutional expression in the conciliar movement (fourteenth century on) that called for reform of the church "in head and members." By the eve of the Reformation, Catholic Humanists and theologians were translating the Bible, preachers were endeavoring to instill piety and ethics, and confraternities and oratories provided vehicles for lay spirituality and charity. The continuation of medieval monastic reforming movements may be seen in Ignatius Loyola (1491–1556), founder of the Society of Jesus (Jesuits), whose interest centered on the promotion of pastoral and mission work rather than the reform of doctrine, and Teresa of Ávila (1515–82), whose mystical writings and work in reforming the Carmelite order remain influential.

On the other hand, the late medieval papacy's antipathy toward conciliarism was a major factor in blocking repeated Protestant calls for a council to deal with the issues raised by the Reformation. When the council finally began in 1546 in Trent, a generation of strife had hardened positions. Mediating efforts – for example, the 1541 Colloquy of Regensburg – had been rejected by both sides as compromises of the "truth."

The Council of Trent, in three distinct assemblies (1545–7, 1551–2, 1561–3), focused on the moral, spiritual, and educational renewal of the Catholic Church, and the refutation of Protestantism. The latter goal found expression in the council's repudiation of *sola scriptura* by stating tradition an equal source of revelation; the supplementation of *sola gratia* with human cooperation; and reaffirmation of the seven sacraments and the doctrine of transubstantiation. Papal authority, although not officially established in the modern sense until Vatican I (1870), was reaffirmed at the conclusion of the Council of Trent by the papal bull *Benedictus Deus* that reserved authentic interpretation of conciliar decrees to the pope.

The Reformations' Aftermath

By the close of the Council of Trent in 1563, Western Christendom was fragmented into "denominations" identified by particular confessions of faith. The hot lava of theological debates and religious innovations that had erupted and flowed over the medieval corpus Christianum solidified into three major communities – Roman Catholicism, Lutheranism, and Reformed Protestantism – each of which had formulated confessions of their beliefs. The consequent intramural and extramural theological conflicts stemmed from each church's effort to consolidate and institutionalize its understanding of the gospel. These efforts have been described under the general term "confessionalization." The confessionalization process was also political and social because all the confessional churches allied themselves with temporal rulers and states to preserve their confessional hegemony and, if possible, extend it to other territories. Non-confessional religious movements such as the Anabaptist and Jewish communities were isolated and marginalized. While on the one hand the confessional churches received legitimacy and support from their respective states, they on the other hand served the development of the modern state by promoting a unified, disciplined society of subjects.

In Protestant states the clergy were integrated into civic life not only by virtue of their participation in marriage and family life, but also by their involvement in the bureaucracy of the state as administrators of the church. In this respect the clergy were civil servants bound by their respective church constitutions and confessions of faith. In Roman Catholic states the administrative structure had similar functions, although it often was more complex. The churches played a significant role in advancing social discipline because they had a legitimacy that the early modern state was still in the process of acquiring in relation to moral, political, and legal norms. Sermons, pastoral care and visitations, religious education through instruction and catechisms, religious services, and the inculcation of discipline promoted the Reformations' sense of vocation in domestic and public affairs. The values of good behavior, honesty, learning, self-discipline, work, and obedience were thereby internalized and provided support for the social and economic transition to the modern European bourgeois society of the industrial age. This so-called "Protestant ethic" was not limited to the Calvinists and their Puritan offspring. Social discipline was a universal expression of confessionalism. For example, the Society of Jesus – the Jesuits – was clearly a meritocracy that rewarded precisely those values esteemed by the developing state and economy: learning, talent, hard work, and piety.

Chapter 9

Pietism and the Enlightenment

Pietism and the Enlightenment usher in a new period of Western Christianity. They may be viewed as siblings, with Pietism the older sister. It is difficult to pinpoint a specific turn from the confessional era to the period of Pietism and the Enlightenment. In the face of the devastation wrought by the religious wars of the Reformation era, capped by the Thirty Years' War (1618–48), it was necessary to begin rebuilding society, a process in which the churches played a role. Politically this is the period from the Peace of Westphalia (1648) to the end of the old Empire (1806). Theologically and philosophically this is the period from Spener's *Pious Desires* (1675) to Kant's *Religion within the Limits of Reason Alone* (1793).

Pietism, the most significant renewal movement since the Reformation, pressed for the individualizing and interiorizing of religious life. Pietism was also a transnational and transconfessional movement wherein Spanish Catholic mysticism influenced English Puritanism and English Puritanism and German Pietism cross-fertilized each other; comparable developments in France were Jansenism and Quietism. The considerable geographical and temporal relationships of these movements combined in implicit and explicit critiques of the establishment churches and prepared the soil for the Enlightenment's call for the emancipation of society from church authorities.

Pietism itself is difficult to define. The name gained currency in the late seventeenth century as a term of abuse and derision. The Pietists themselves, however, accepted the description provided in a poem of the time composed for the funeral of a pious theology student: "What is a Pietist? One who studies God's Word, and also lives a holy life according to it." In brief, then, Pietism as a movement was marked by intense study of the Bible and a focus on sanctification. It was also a strong lay movement. Its participants' diaries and autobiographies focused on conversion and inner life, and are the forerunners of modern, psychological introspection and analysis. Pietism was transdenominational not only in terms of the influences spreading from Roman Catholic mysticism through Puritan devotional literature to Lutheran piety, but also in its ecumenism of religious experience over doctrine. Indeed, one may argue that Pietism so focused on religious experience that it not only transcended, but also undermined the churches' confessions. Hence, Philipp Jakob Spener (1635–1705), the "Father of Pietism," has also been referred to as an impetus for theological liberalism. It is perhaps no accident that the major figures of the Enlightenment – Lessing, Kant, Schiller, Goethe, Fichte, and Schleiermacher – came from Pietist backgrounds. In a sense then, Pietism's efforts to protect the Christian faith from modernity by turning to experience reflected that very modernity. Pietism's borders have always been permeable – both theologically and chronologically. Theologically, the Pietist emphasis upon religious experience and holy living eroded confessional demarcations between Lutheran Orthodoxy, Reformed Puritanism, and Roman Catholicism, and stimulated the early Rationalism and Enlightenment of the Baroque period. Chronologically, the roots of Pietism extend back through such Reformation "enthusiasts" as Karlstadt and Müntzer into medieval mystical spiritualism and forward to modern charismatic movements. Furthermore, the influence of Pietism continues through its devotional writings and hymnody; most modern hymnbooks contain numerous hymns from the period of Pietism.

Faced by the complexity of Pietism, we shall take a very simple path leading from Arndt to Spener to Francke. We begin with Johann Arndt (1555–1621) not only because of his incredible influence but also because he exemplifies the positive connection of Pietism and Protestant Orthodoxy. It is not uncommon to find Pietism described as a reaction to Orthodoxy's fight for right belief during the post-Reformation confessional age. The Pietists' penchant for sloganeering no doubt contributes to this perspective. Their emphasis that the Christian life is a walk not a talk, a becoming not being, that heart religion opposes head religion, and that life is over doctrine, was succinctly summed up by the radical Pietist Christian Hoburg (1606–75), who stated: "Justification is fiction, rebirth is fact." In less extreme formulations, the moderate Pietists affirmed the continuation of the Reformation of doctrine by the Reformation of life. Arndt expressed this theme in the foreword to his immensely popular *Four Books on True Christianity*: "It is not enough to know God's word; one must also practice it in a living, active manner." Arndt's writings were so popular that their hundreds of editions overshadowed Luther's influence in the seventeenth and eighteenth centuries, and his *True Christianity* was reprinted in America by Benjamin Franklin.

Arndt addressed a different context than had Luther. Luther's proclamation of justification by grace alone through faith, the good news that salvation is received not achieved, addressed late medieval people who sought salvation by good works, pilgrimages, and indulgences. Thanks to the acceptance of that message, people's religious interest turned to the consequences of justification. What follows from faith? The emphasis shifted from justification to sanctification and rebirth, to the pious life.

Arndt wrote to supplement justifying faith, not to critique it. Nevertheless, he initiated a piety of interiority and introspection.

While Luther in his Small Catechism petitioned that the Kingdom of God may come *to* us, Arndt spoke of the Kingdom that will be established *in* us. Arndt's interiority did not lead to passivity and quietism. His emphasis on active, living faith stimulated a major renewal movement based upon practical Christianity. Johann Amos Comenius (1592–1670), the bishop of the Moravian Brethren and the most significant reform educator of the early modern period, reckoned himself among the students of Arndt. And Johann Valentin Andreä (1586–1654) dedicated his *Christianopolis* (1619), the first utopian social novel in Lutheran Germany, to Johann Arndt. Andreä pictured an ideal Christian social order developed upon platonic-communistic foundations, and took steps to institutionalize it. His Färber-Stift – founded in 1621 as a foundation for the poor, supported by citizens enriched by cloth-dying – is among the oldest social institutions of the early bourgeois period. After the Thirty Years' War, Andreä introduced in the Württemberg church the Calvinist church discipline he had learned in Geneva. However, the attempt failed because the nobility evaded moral supervision. Andreä lamented lazy Lutheran preachers whose ideal was "short sermons and long bratwursts." He increasingly viewed the "new papacy" of the state-controlled church as the strongest obstacle to any moral improvement.

These developments occurred in the context of the general deterioration of living conditions after 1600 culminating in the Thirty Years' War. The war undermined the unity of church and society. Furthermore, princely absolutism and the seeds of the Enlightenment began to emancipate political and intellectual life from the power of the confessional church bodies and their theological traditions.

The profound upheaval of the war cannot be underestimated. There is no doubt that rural populations suffered the most. City walls provided some protection from the fury of the conflicts, whereas rural towns and villages were totally unprotected. After that war, there was renewed war with the Turks. The Tatars invaded East Prussia in 1656–7 with the loss of some 100,000. In 1709 the plague returned and extended as far as Berlin, carrying away some 155,000. Under these drastic conditions the rural population largely withdrew from the spiritual and political life of the country. The bourgeoisie also had difficult lives. Tradesmen were increasingly oppressed by the rising money economy. And the large numbers of unemployed soldiers contributed to widespread begging and unrest.

Social distinctions were emphasized as never before. The nobles expressed their attitude toward the lower classes by creating physical boundaries. They insulated their homes by parks and iron fences, and their churches by separate areas for prayer and worship. At the Lord's Supper people came up according to class. The parish community reflected the social order of the secular society, and for the lower classes the church was a place of humiliation just like their everyday existence. One no longer spoke of the universal priesthood of the baptized, and the distinction between clergy and laity was reemphasized by the increasing separation of the clerical office from the people. The worst conditions in the cities fell on the laborers in the new manufacturing industries, especially the textile workers. The sharpening of class differences within church and society led to increasing criticism of the churches, which appeared ineffectual in ameliorating social conditions. Separation from the church and a homegrown atheism reached its high point between 1690 and 1730, and in turn stimulated a spate of reform proposals.

It was in this context that Spener presented a "theology of hope" that proclaimed a better future based upon the renewal of society through renewal of the church. In contrast to pessimism concerning the future fostered by the crises of the time, Spener spoke of the coming great time of mission possibilities to the whole world, of Judaism's turn to Christianity, and an overcoming of the Counter-Reformation.

Spener's *Pious Desires or heartfelt desire for a God-pleasing improvement of the true evangelical church* appeared in 1675 as the foreword to a new edition of Arndt's sermons. The church's lack of true, living faith was to be countered by bringing God's Word more fully into the church and world through reading and discussing the Bible in devotional assemblies. Thus Pietism became a Bible movement that strove to activate the universal priesthood of all believers (or at least all the reborn), shift the focus from the theory to the praxis of Christianity, limit confessional polemics, reform theological studies in the sense of the practice of piety, and finally redirect preaching to the edification and cultivation of the "inner man." Spener believed the improvement of the church possible for God promised a splendid future for his church.

The *Pious Desires* became the programmatic writing of Pietism. Spener desired to reform the church through the cultivation of the pious. Among other things, he demanded the revival of the universal priesthood and the freedom for lay activity in the church. The laity should have the opportunity to gather together with the clergy for common Bible study. The people are not to be "objects" of sermons and pastoral activity, but "subjects" to be involved in practicing Christianity by means of the meditative appropriation of the whole Bible. Meditation was also promoted as the means for personal application of the sermon, and for contemporizing the events of the Passion in relation to the Lord's Supper. The formation of voluntary circles within the church, known as the *ecclesiola in ecclesia* ("the little church in the church"), would be the avant-garde for the inbreaking Kingdom of God. At the same time, Spener guarded against the inclination to flee the world through his emphasis upon an active Christianity.

Spener's Pietism placed within Protestantism an active social-political will. In 1666, as the senior pastor in Frankfurt, he re-ordered the city's program of poor relief. He soon became widely known, and Frederick III in 1693 sought his opinion on reducing the widespread begging in Berlin. In one generation, Berlin had grown from about 30,000 to 50,000. Among this expanded population there were numerous discharged soldiers, widows, and orphans. The social need was indescribable; women and their daughters entered prostitution in countless numbers. Spener's plan was to use almsgiving to establish work places. Invalids, widows, and orphans should be cared for in humane fashion in public institutions, without regard to their class and denomination. The financing of social programs was by weekly door-to-door collections, and state subsidies for the discharged soldiers. In 1695 Frederick created a central poor relief fund, and in 1702 the Grosse Friedrichshospital arose, from which developed the Berlin Charité, an orphanage, and an insane asylum. Within two years after establishment, it was already supporting some 2,000 people.

Spener became head court preacher in Dresden in 1686, the highest clerical position in Protestant Germany. In 1691 he was called to Berlin where, protected by the Brandenburg-Prussian state, he defended the Pietist movement against the attacks of the Orthodox. He was able to place his Pietist friends and students in key positions of church and academic life. The far-reaching Pietist character of Halle University (established in 1694) was due to his influence as well as that of his young follower, August Hermann Francke (1663–1727). As a true patriarch of Pietism, Spener died in 1705 in Berlin viewed as the second greatest theologian in Lutheranism after Luther.

Francke – preacher and pastor, theologian and educator, incredible organizer – spent more than three decades developing the most historically significant form of Pietism, Halle Pietism. As a student he had experienced a sudden life-determining conversion after days of inner struggle. It made him certain of God's existence and his own rebirth. The importance of a sudden, datable, and one-time conversion – still alien to Spener – entered Pietism through Francke.

Through Spener's influence, Francke received an academic post as professor of Oriental languages in the new Prussian University of Halle and a pastoral charge in the Halle suburb of Glaucha. There he initiated pastoral and social programs that became legendary. The "Franckean Institutions" included an orphanage, training schools for teachers and pastors, various schools for different levels and classes of students, a *collegium orientale* for scripture study and translation, a publishing house, a science laboratory, and an apothecary. Francke titled his own account of these developments *The Footprints of the Still-Living God* (1701–9). This classic defense of Pietism was printed in English with the Latinized title *Pietas Hallensis* (1727) and influenced both the British Isles and the Atlantic coast of colonial North America. Some of Francke's writings were published in America, and the Boston Puritan Cotton Mather (1663–1728) carried on an extensive correspondence with Francke.

Francke's entrepreneurial ability enabled him to initiate the above-mentioned Institutions with only the few dollars he found left in his parish poor box and then raise the funds for an imposing series of Baroque buildings. He contributed a social advance in separating the orphanage from the poorhouse, the workhouse, and the house of correction. The orphanage itself was the most advanced of its time. Among other things it was a pioneer of modern hygiene. At a time when few took offense at bodily uncleanness, Francke and his colleagues insisted that children brush their teeth, bathe, and have clean clothes and bedding. Here, cleanliness was indeed next to godliness.

The reform of theological studies at Halle soon made it the most frequented faculty for theology students in all Germany, and then a center for foreign missions that extended to America in the West and Russia and India in the East. The study of theology was tied directly to praxis. For example, theology students interned in the hospital. They also learned rudimentary medical and pharmacological skills that, as the Halle missionary to America, Henry Melchior Muhlenberg (1711–87) learned, stood them in good stead in their missionary work. Francke introduced studies into his schools with the motto that a Christian "shall be equipped and sent out so that all the world may see that no more useful people may be found than those who belong to Jesus Christ."

Francke viewed holy living as serious business, and warned against unnecessary laughter at jokes and foolish things that distract the mind. His *Rules for Living* condemned laziness and stressed hard work and obedience to authority. His critique of luxury prohibited spending time on one's appearance, looking in the mirror, or being concerned for finery and jewelry. Francke's emphasis upon introspection is evident in his mandate for constant, diligent self-examination. In lines reminiscent of Loyola's *Spiritual Exercises* Francke exhorted his readers not to weary in examining their consciences. Works, words, desires, and ideas are to be scrutinized. Ideas and thoughts are to be controlled because "a child can more easily stamp out a spark than a hundred men can extinguish a raging fire."

Pietism's strongest moral influence was upon the ethics of the bourgeoisie. As Francke emphasized in his tracts on educating youth, the three central virtues of a God-pleasing life are love of the truth, obedience, and diligence. These virtues of industriousness, thrift, and obedience were obviously pleasing to early modern states. Precisely as demanders of bourgeois virtues the Pietists often found themselves at least indirectly to be supporters of state powers. The alliance of Pietism and the Prussian state occurred under the "Soldier-King" Friedrich Wilhelm I (1713–40). After some hesitation, Francke placed himself in the service of the Prussian state. His Institutions served to create industrious state servants, and Pietism gained special access to the army by providing field chaplains. The most important result of this symbiosis of state authority and piety was the obedient, conscientious, diligent, and selfless civil servant as represented especially in the ethos of the Prussian bureaucracy and officer corps.

Halle Pietism also echoed themes of English devotional literature that presented the ideal of individual praxis-oriented piety in a thoroughly rationalized, psychologically reflective manner relevant to the time's new drive toward analysis, order, and goal-directed thinking. English devotional literature was not confessional-specific but sought to concretize the ideal of the Christian life and make it feasible.

In England as in Germany the new conception of piety promoted personal meditation. One of the most influential devotional works was Lewis Bayly's (d. 1631) *Practice of Piety*. By 1636 it had gone through at least 36 editions in English, and by 1628 a German edition with the Latinized title *Praxis Pietatis* also went through many editions. The greater part of English devotional literature focused on sanctification, including denial of the self and contempt of the world in order to master the Christian's everyday life.

The rules of life are impressively concrete. Reflecting the contemporary fascination with natural science, especially the uncovering of hidden pathologies by the science of anatomy, the Christian life was anatomized into a network of individual rules that regulated the course of the day and especially the hallowing of Sunday. *Praxis Pietatis* meant the "systematic practice" of the Christian life. Richard Baxter (1615–91) exhorted his readers to think not only of consoling words but also to practice the rules he gave them. Practice brings advance in sanctification. When the motive of the pilgrim is evoked, then it comprehends not only the Christian's alienation from the earth but above all his goal-directedness: the Pilgrim's Progress.

The seventeenth century began with the ideal of a uniform state church reflective on a small scale of the old ideal of the corpus Christianum. But that ideal was not sustainable. States and cultures increasingly emancipated themselves from ecclesiastical control, and looked to standards derived from the "nature" of human life and society. Baroque music, for example, began shifting from worship settings to concert halls. The reverse also occurred, and thereby raised anxieties about secular incursion into sacred space and time. In brief, the pluralism initiated, although not intended, by the Reformation was becoming more and more apparent. There were now alternative modes of living and understanding life. What did this mean for Christians who now spent a good portion of their lives in the non-churchly aspects of this developing culture? What could that "Christianity" be that was not the standard and the motive for the whole life of the Christian?

Pietism provided a provisional and, it turned out, a less than helpful answer: the individualization and internalization of the faith. Cultural development and fragmentation could be ignored by seeking religious fellowship with the like-minded; by personal appropriation of religious truth that was no longer accepted as universal; by subjective religious experience and personal devotion and discipline. The downside of this orientation was the segregation of a certain sphere of life as religious, with the rest of life being secular by default. Pietists might lament this state of affairs, but adherents of the Enlightenment rejoiced in it and sought to expand it. In the process the Enlightenment was also heir to some of the fundamental emphases of Pietism: an anthropocentric orientation to religion rooted in personal experience, an orientation toward a better future, and a concern for morality that could be inculcated through education.

The Enlightenment

Unlike previous eras that looked back to classical culture or early Christianity, the Enlightenment was optimistically oriented toward the future in terms of continuing improvement. The modern Swiss theologian Karl Barth (1886–1968) described this period in terms of "absolutism" and the "desire for form." This may be seen in the popular use of plaster in Baroque architecture and the mastery of form in music from Bach to Mozart, as well as new theories of nature that dispensed with the God-hypothesis for scientific explanations. Alexander Pope (1688–1744) succinctly expressed the new orientation with this dictum:

"The proper study of mankind is man." Confidence in human capability found novelistic expression in Daniel Defoe's (1660–1731) *Robinson Crusoe*, whose hero masters nature and life when thrown back on his own resources. The conviction that the mastery of nature and human life resided in education led to a number of Enlightenment treatises, such as Gotthold Ephraim Lessing's (1729–81) *The Education of the Human Race*, Jean-Jacques Rousseau's (1712–78) *Émile, or Treatise on Education*, and Johann Heinrich Pestalozzi's (1746–1827) *How Gertrude Teaches Her Children*. These found pragmatic expression in the rise of teacher training schools. Immanuel Kant (1724–1804), the culmination of Enlightenment philosophy, himself defined the Enlightenment as "the emergence from a self-inflicted state of minority," and challenged his contemporaries to think for themselves, to "have the courage to make use of your own understanding."

Kant's summary definition of the Enlightenment capped a European-wide development. René Descartes (1596–1650), educated by the Jesuits, expressed the modern self-consciousness rooted in reason: *cogito ergo sum* – I think therefore I am! The existence of God becomes rational, and philosophy shifts from its role as the "handmaid of theology" (Aquinas) to a fundamental scientific discipline founded on empirical observations and rational principles. In England, Deism sought a firm foundation for religious propositions so that any person of sound mind and common sense could accept them. Edward Lord Herbert of Cherbury (1581–1648) reduced Christianity to five "reasonable" points: God exists; God is to be served; such service is a matter of morality not ritual; mistakes are to be regretted and made good; ethical living merits reward here and hereafter. Christianity was being reduced to God, moral freedom, and immortality. John Locke (1632–1704) understood Christianity in terms of tolerance, virtue, and morality, and wrote *The Reasonableness of Christianity as Delivered in the Scriptures*.

The drive toward the harmony of reason and revelation reflected battle fatigue from religious controversies; if Christianity could be reduced to reasonable essentials then causes of conflict could be removed. Theological reductionism was also a reflection of the growing awareness of the diversity of the world's religions. The Bible as the record of revelation transcending reason and nature was increasingly questioned. This shift is expressed in two important writings: John Toland's (1670–1722) *Christianity not Mysterious* and Matthew Tindal's (1655–1733) *Christianity as Old as the Creation, or the Gospel a Republication of the Religion of Nature*. The latter became the "Bible" of Deism, and was translated into German. Since Christianity contains nothing mysterious in opposition to human reason, then the miracle stories and resurrection reports are open to criticism.

The effort to reduce Christianity to reasonableness was dealt a major blow by the Scottish empiricist David Hume (1711–76), who was equally critical of metaphysics and theology on the basis that knowledge comes from sense experience and can be shown to be correct only when tested against further experience. In response to the appeal to an inherent religious sense, Hume noted that the earliest forms of religion were not archetypes of English civilization but gross anthropomorphic polytheisms. Primitive gods were mysterious, tricky beings who fell notably short of the moral conduct of humans. Hume's final critique of religion was an ethical one. Religion directs human attention away from life, and preoccupation with salvation is apt to make persons narrow and bigoted. Hume suggested the wise person avoid the disputes of the theologians provided he can make himself immune to their rancor and persecution.

In France, François-Marie Voltaire (1694–1778) used the concepts of English Deism to fight against the Catholic Church. His sharp wit made him a controversial figure. He generally rejected philosophical theories for God, but thought God remained an important presupposition for moral order and the prevention of anarchy. It is in this sense that his famous comment should be read: "If God did not exist, it would be necessary to invent him."

Fascination with the natural sciences – also a preoccupation among leading Pietists, who with their age saw "experience" and "experiment" as synonyms – found expression in the *Encyclopedia* (35 volumes) edited by Denis Diderot (1713–84) and Jean d'Alembert (ca. 1717–83). This monumental digest of eighteenth-century rationalism mediated Enlightenment ideas to the French bourgeoisie, including Francis Bacon's (1561–1626) view that human rule over nature would advance history on the path of freedom and human happiness. Rousseau posited that the future of humankind resides not in reason but the powers and feelings of the natural man, hence the alleged motto "back to nature." Persons are born good but society, culture, the state, and religion pervert humankind's naturally good faculties. Rousseau influenced others through his *The Social Contract*, which presented an ideal, natural order of the state as a democracy served by civil religion. Thus Rousseau has been regarded as a spiritual father of the French Revolution.

In Germany the Enlightenment was less critical toward the state and the church, perhaps because it coexisted with as well as derived from Pietism. Gottfried Wilhelm Leibnitz (1646–1716) emphasized that faith and reason may harmoniously coexist. He addressed the problem of theodicy, the justification of God in the face of evil in the world, by his thesis that our world is "the best of all possible worlds." Evil is based in the restrictedness of finite being. But reason may recognize the good and the divine as the essential structure of the world. Leibnitz's optimistic view of the world conceives of sin only as the imperfect good. However, the Lisbon earthquake (1755) that destroyed the city and tens of thousands of people severely shook his confidence that this is the best of all possible worlds. Voltaire's pessimistic *Candide* (1759) ends with the advice to retire to one's garden and withdraw from the horrors of history.

Since revelation had become suspect, Enlightenment theologians generally strove to depict Christianity in social-ethical terms. Hence, Jesus became the great teacher of wisdom and virtue, the forerunner of the Enlightenment who broke the bonds of error (not sin!) and served as a model for humankind. The Enlightenment also raised critical questions for the churches, not least of which concerned biblical authorship and Christian origins. Hermann Samuel Reimarus (1694–1768) claimed these origins were fraudulent. He viewed Jesus as a failed political messiah whose resurrection was fabricated by the disciples to counter their disappointment and to gain recognition in the world. Reimarus' arguments were published by Gotthold Ephraim Lessing (1729–81) with the (mistaken!) rationale that they would stimulate constructive discussion of the meaning of Christianity. Lessing's own position is summarized in his famous line: "The accidental truths of history can never be the proof for the necessary truths of reason." In other words, historical testimony of revelation cannot provide certainty of its truth. Historical religions, he argued, are stages of a divine process of education toward the true religion of love and reason. In Lessing's *Nathan the Wise* there is the parable of the ring where the true ring cannot be distinguished from two perfect imitations; hence each of the three heirs should live as if the father's true ring was given to him. The truth of real religion is manifest in its experience and practice.

The reduction of Christianity to morality "peaked" in Immanuel Kant. Nurtured in Pietism, he went off to a Pietist school at the age of eight. There he encountered Pietism's dark side: hypocrisy. It has been suggested that this context instilled in him such an abhorrence of religious emotion that he avoided church services altogether. A famous account relates that when made rector of the University of Königsberg he led the customary academic procession to the cathedral for the inauguration of rectors, but deserted the procession at the church. He was born and reared in Königsberg, attended the university there, became professor of philosophy there, and died there without ever going outside the borders of the province – clearly a challenge to the old adage that travel broadens the mind!

Kant provided the classic definition of the Enlightenment as the emergence from a self-inflicted state of minority. A minor is one who is incapable of understanding without guidance from someone else. This minority is self-inflicted whenever its cause lies in a lack of determination and courage to make use of one's reason without the supervision of another. Dare to use your own understanding is therefore the watchword of the Enlightenment. Kant championed autonomy, but did not mean doing whatever one pleases. Rather, true autonomy – self-law – is obedience to the universal law of reason. This is what makes Kant's age, as he says, the true age of criticism. Everything must be subjected to criticism. Every form of heteronomy (i.e., authorities external to the person that compromise autonomy, whether parents, society, state, church, or understandings of God) must be critiqued. Reason itself may not be excluded from criticism in order that in its critical use reason can be sure of itself.

Kant based religion as a moral system on his maxim "I ought, therefore I can." A person cannot be held responsible unless capable of doing something about his or her situation. Every sensible person will realize that the experience of oughtness leads to the moral mandates: "Treat every person as an end not as a means," and "Act solely on that principle which could become a universal law governing everyone's actions." The latter is known as the "categorical imperative." Faith is understood in terms of the duty to fulfill one's knowledge of the good. Pure religious faith, that is, morality, has no need for the church. The title of Kant's work on religion summarizes his viewpoint: *Religion within the Limits of Reason Alone.*

In limiting Christianity to reason, Kant inverted the order of the Reformation. Instead of good works flowing from grace, Kant begins with good works and reads all theological subjects in this light. Hence, Christ is viewed not as the Redeemer but as the moral archetype or model of the godly life to be imitated by humankind. Instead of God's descent to humankind, humankind is to ascend to God's commands. Autonomy is destroyed by anything applied from outside the self, including the grace of God. If God forgives; if God has mercy on whom he wills, then humankind is not free. Kant takes the side of Pelagius in the old battle over grace and free will. The one fly in Kant's ointment was the problem of "radical evil," which he acknowledged he could not resolve. But if evil is radical, it is also irrational, and there goes reason alone. This was shocking to Kant's Enlightenment contemporaries, whose optimistic rational concepts of God and humankind excluded sin and evil. Hence Goethe's pithy comment summarized the reaction of the day: in speaking of radical evil, Kant "slobbered" on his philosophical mantle.

The Catholic Church and the Enlightenment

In general, the Roman Catholic Church and its theologians were far less open to the Enlightenment than Protestant theologians. To the Roman Catholic Magisterium (teaching authority), in particular, the Enlightenment appeared as the destruction of Christendom. In the first half of the eighteenth century there were still a few late actions in the spirit of the Counter-Reformation: The "church of the wilderness" (Camisards or "French prophets," fanatical, ecstatic French Calvinists) was persecuted by Louis XIV in France, and evangelicals were expelled from the archbishopric of Salzburg in 1731. Also the Jansenist (a Catholic reforming movement) controversy broke out again, and led to another papal condemnation. Jesuit influences and pressures for orthodoxy unleashed such a storm of outrage in France, Portugal, and Spain that pope Clement XIV suspended the Jesuit order in 1773.

The concept of "Josephinism" showed however that the Enlightenment had also penetrated into the Catholic Church. The Austrian ruler Joseph II (r. 1780–90) attempted to bring the church under the rule of Enlightenment absolutism. This meant complete independence of the Austrian Catholic Church from Rome, reduction of the number of monasteries, reform of the theological formation of the clergy, and simplification of worship in the sense of a rational-ethical piety. Toleration (1781) gave Protestants the same civil rights as Catholics, as well as the right to exercise religion. This national church effort at reform was later withdrawn.

In Germany the bishoprics of the Rhine and Würzburg grasped the spirit of the Enlightenment and directed a popular reform Catholicism and an episcopacy independent of Rome. A book by the Trier suffragan bishop Johann Nikolaus von Hontheim (1701–90) under the pseudonym Justinius Febronius claimed that only the council of bishops, not the pope, is infallible; papal primacy is only a primacy of honor; and that the German Catholic Church should be independent of Rome. In 1786 the archbishop-electors summarized and again asserted these reform demands, but without success. Disunity among the bishops, lack of support from the Catholic state, and the outbreak of the French Revolution led to the victory of the papacy over Febronianism.

Chapter 10

Challenge and Response: The Church in the Nineteenth Century

Historians sometimes conceptualize the nineteenth century as the "long century" that begins with the French Revolution (1789) and concludes with the outbreak of World War I (1914). Parallel events in the history of theology are the Romantic affirmation of liberalism in Friedrich Schleiermacher's (1768–1834) *On Religion: Speeches to its Cultured Despisers* (1799) and the rejection of liberal theology in Karl Barth's (1886–1968) *Romans Commentary* (1918).

In general, nineteenth-century developments put the churches on the defensive. The Enlightenment and the rise of the natural sciences challenged biblical revelation and the foundations of the faith. Ludwig Feuerbach (1804–72) questioned the existence of God, and had the audacity to claim that theology, "the queen of the sciences," had no clothes when he stated that theology is anthropology. David Friedrich Strauss (1808–74) questioned the historicity of Jesus and described the Son of God as a myth. And for those who heeded Karl Marx's (1818–83) clarion call to socialism, that myth was not benign but an opiate that fogged the minds of the masses. In addition, the social consequences of the French and the industrial revolutions called into serious question the churches' relevance to society and culture.

It appeared to the churches that the barbarians were at the gates. In general, the Roman Catholic response was to lock the gates as securely as possible; to shut out the modern world if it could not be destroyed. The Protestant churches were not immune to this temptation – the rise of fundamentalism is a case in point – but also attempted to dialogue with the barbarians. These dialogical efforts became preoccupied with trying to ascertain the "essence" of Christianity in order to demonstrate that in its core the Christian faith was not antithetical to the modern world but rather supported the best it had to offer. On the social level, both the Catholic and Protestant churches promoted the faith through a variety of associations that ministered to the manifold needs of those wounded by the upheavals of the times.

The Churches and the French Revolution

The French Revolution promoted the ideas of popular sovereignty and democracy and the concepts of liberty, fraternity, and equality. People responded with either enthusiastic agreement or suffering dissent. On the one hand, political aspirations going back to medieval conciliarism sought political-social realization. On the other hand, the advance of the Revolution called forth multiple counter-reactions that pressed for the restoration of pre-revolutionary conditions. The Revolution furthermore accelerated the long history of criticism of the churches' influence. Pietism and the Enlightenment provided a strong practical and conceptual impetus for these developments, but it is in the nineteenth century that secularism proceeded beyond the upper middle class and created the modern context of the church.

Industrialization also profoundly changed the lives of people in the cities and the countryside. Charles Dickens vividly portrayed the degradation of urban living conditions in social novels such as *Oliver Twist* (1838) and *David Copperfield* (1850). The rise of a worker-proletariat and the rapid growth of cities created unimaginable problems, and consequently the modern mass collective that in socialist movements strove for power and its share of the communal pie.

The churches found themselves in a struggle to retain at least influence if not control over schools, marriage, public morality, nationalism, and science. By and large, nationalists and secularists did not desire to kill the churches but to conform them to the rationale of the state, and to establish reason over revelation for the common interest of society. Even those who emphasized churchly authority as the guarantee of tradition and legitimacy did so for reasons of state and strove to prohibit the churches from expressing political interests. Monarchs throughout Europe repeatedly emphasized that, as Wilhelm II of Prussia put it, "pastors ought to attend to the souls of the faithful and cultivate charity, but let politics alone for it does not concern them."

From the French Revolution to the Congress of Vienna

The Roman Catholic Church, profoundly tied to the old regime, shared to a great extent the fate of the absolute state in the French Revolution. For the first time in Europe the centuries-old connection of church and state was dissolved. The earlier American war of independence also separated church and state, but not by antagonism to the church. There Christianity and the free churches were rather an important factor for the people and politics.

The French National Assembly (1789–92) secularized church property, dissolved monasteries, and provided the "Civil Constitution for the Clergy." The latter subordinated church administration to the state; placed election of bishops and priests with the citizens; determined clerical income; released clergy from obedience to foreign authority (the papacy!); and demanded an oath of loyalty to the nation and constitution by all the clergy. During the Reign of Terror (1793–4) the government abolished the Christian calendar, prohibited Christian festivals, declared marriage a purely civil concern, pillaged and destroyed many churches, and set up the cult of reason in place of worship.

Napoleon Bonaparte restored the Catholic Church in the Concordat of 1801. The Catholic Church was recognized as the majority church of the French, but remained subordinate to state oversight. In 1804 Napoleon had pope Pius VII come to France to crown him emperor. At the ceremony, Napoleon overturned the tradition that had begun with the crowning of Charlemagne in 800 – he took the crown from the pope's hands and crowned himself! Popes no longer "made" emperors. In 1809 France incorporated the Papal States. Pius responded by excommunicating Napoleon, who then imprisoned the pope. Pius' resistance during these "troubles" contributed to the enhancement of papal prestige after the fall of Napoleon in 1815.

Prussia was drawn into the maelstrom of change through the coalition war against France, but was defeated at Jena and Auerstadt. French influence now led to the introduction of the Napoleonic Code, a collection of civil legislation that included civil equality, freedom of religion, equality of the confessions, and a non-confessional state. However, national and liberal reform movements were shoved aside by the new political order created at the Congress of Vienna (1815). State and church sought mutual support – the so-called alliance of "Throne and Altar" – and efforts were made to thwart constitutional and national aspirations. The repressed desires for reforms, however, broke out in numerous uprisings – the July Revolution in France in 1830 and the 1848 revolutions in Switzerland, France, and Prussia.

Church Reform in Germany: The Prussian Union and its Consequences

The cataclysms of the Revolution and the Napoleonic era forced continual reorganization of the churches. Prussia, predominantly

Lutheran, now also included a number of Reformed territories whose confessional commitments had to be taken seriously. On the personal level, the Reformed ruler Frederick Wilhelm III (1770–1840) was married to a Lutheran and wanted to share communion with her. The 300th anniversary of Luther's "Ninety-five Theses" in 1817 provided what the crown thought to be an appropriate occasion for uniting the two major Reformation churches. But widespread clergy opposition arose when the king intervened in affairs of the churches and mandated uniformity of worship according to his own liturgical creation. In opposition to the Prussian Union thousands of Lutherans emigrated to North America and Australia. A cabinet order of 1834 granted the Lutheran and Reformed churches continuing existence as specific confessions, and thus the Prussian Union brought forth three Protestant communities: Lutheran, Reformed, and United; a unified Union Church did not develop.

Inner Mission and the Social Question

The Francke Institutions at Halle, Pietism's efforts to transform the world by transforming individuals, were forerunners of nineteenth-century Protestant efforts to respond to social issues through the Inner Mission (i.e., service within the country in distinction from foreign mission) and the deaconess movements. These two movements soon became interrelated and addressed the same social miseries that called forth Marx's famous "Manifesto." The major figures of the Inner Mission and the development of the female diaconate are, respectively, Johann Hinrich Wichern (1808–81) and Theodore Fliedner (1800–64).

Wichern, a Hamburg pastor stunned by the impoverishment of the masses, began rescue homes for neglected and delinquent children. His initial effort, begun in 1833, emphasized education and job training in the context of God's forgiving grace. He then enlisted and trained assistants for this work, initiating what would become deacon and deaconess training institutes. In 1844 he began publishing a newspaper to arouse social conscience. Wichern was concerned that the future of both Christianity and society was jeopardized by the growing alienation of the urban masses from a seemingly uncaring state church. In 1848, some months after the appearance of Marx's "Communist Manifesto" and the outbreak of revolution in Berlin, Wichern issued a "Protestant Manifesto" at a meeting of the evangelical churches in Wittenberg.

In this long (2 hours!) rhetorical *tour de force*, Wichern proclaimed "love no less than faith is the church's indispensable mark." The church would have a future if it would only incarnate God's love in the industrialized cities. His forceful speech led to the formation of the Central Committee of Inner Missions of the German Evangelical Church.

"Redeeming love" was to awaken the whole society, and transform the church from an authoritarian establishment into a fellowship in which the laity would rediscover its mission as the universal priesthood to respond to the spiritual and social plight of society. The chief aims of the Inner Mission included reclaiming those who had left the church, and assisting the needy, sick, and poor. Wichern's initial advocacy for self-help associations broadened to include prison reform as well as care for the homeless, the mentally and physically disabled, immigrants, and seamen. The Inner Mission soon spread to other European countries and to America. It eventually became an umbrella agency for a wide variety of activities including social welfare work and services.

Wichern's work was not, of course, an isolated expression of Christian faith. Throughout Europe at this time religious renewal movements inspired social concern for the masses of people pauperized by industrialization. The Methodists in England had long been laboring at adult education, schooling, reform of prisons, abolition of slavery, and aid to alcoholics. Famous missions arose in Basel, London, and Paris. The YMCA (1844), YWCA

(1855), and Salvation Army (1865) were only some of the numerous Christian efforts to respond to the ills of modern society.

The revival of Christian service came not only through the Inner Mission, but also through the development of the deaconess movement by the German pastors Fliedner and Wilhelm Loehe (1808–72) who, among others, greatly desired the renewal of a women's ministry in the church.

In 1823 one of the precursors of the deaconess movement, Amalie Sieveking (1794–1859), began a sisterhood analogous to the Roman Catholic Sisters of Charity. During the 1831 Hamburg cholera epidemic she appealed to others to join her in nursing the sick. Undeterred by the lack of response, she carried on to become the director of the cholera hospital. In 1832 she organized a women's society for the care of the sick and the poor in Hamburg that served as an inspiration to Fliedner.

Fliedner's first steps toward the development of the female diaconate began with work on behalf of prisoners inspired by the English Quaker Elizabeth Fry (1780–1845) and the Mennonite deaconess movement he had observed in Holland. In 1833 a discharged woman prisoner came to the Fliedner parsonage in Kaiserswerth for help. The Fliedners lodged her in their garden house. Thus began the famous Kaiserswerth Institutions. Other discharged women prisoners as well as women in need began arriving, and the Fliedners trained them to serve others. The first Protestant deaconess motherhouse, established in Kaiserswerth in 1836, provided a structured environment of mutual support and a training center. Their ministry extended beyond helping released prisoners to serving the sick, orphans, and others at the margins of society. This is the origin of the Rhenish-Westphalian Deaconess Association, a model for dozens of similar associations that sprang up throughout Europe. By 1884 there were 56 deaconess communities with 5,653 deaconesses.

In addition to training deaconesses, the Fliedners also trained salaried Christian nurses. The experience of the pioneer English nurse Florence Nightingale (1820–1910) at Kaiserswerth informed her service in the Crimean War and the shape of her own school of nursing. By that time deaconesses from Kaiserswerth were serving in hospitals in England, America, Jerusalem, Constantinople, and Alexandria.

Loehe, Fliedner's contemporary, established a deaconess house in Neuendettelsau based on his conviction that Christian service flowed from fellowship grounded in the eucharistic liturgy. He organized a society for Inner Mission, and promoted foreign missions as well. The Neuendettelsau Foreign Mission Society trained people for work in America, Australia, and Brazil, and continues to this day.

The Inner Mission and diaconal movements increasingly came to understand the role that economic and social conditions such as work environments, unemployment, underemployment, and discrimination played among people the church sought to serve. Thus there was growing sensitivity to the view that diaconal work must encompass the political as well as the personal and congregational realms. One of the pastors who responded to these concerns was Rudolf Todt (1839–87). His *Radical German Socialism and Christian Society* agreed with the socialist analysis of class struggle, industrial exploitation of workers, social alienation, and mass poverty. He viewed proletarian revolt as legitimate emancipation from oppression, but advocated reform over revolution. Although he shocked many of his clerical contemporaries, and Bismarck considered banning his writings, Todt's National Association for Social Reform and its newspaper did help prepare the way for later social legislation.

Another challenge to the alliance of throne and altar came from a young pastor in an industrial parish in Saxony, Friedrich Naumann (1860–1919), who had worked with Wichern. Naumann and his colleagues opposed any form of Christian paternalism, and desired to work with social democrats to develop a party of radical reform. Bitter controversies resulted, and by the 1890s the Christian socialists of the Naumann school were denounced not only by Kaiser Wilhelm II but also by the Prussian Protestant church. Pastors were told to stay out of politics. Naumann himself resigned from the ministry, entered politics, and in 1919 participated in drafting the Weimar constitution as a member of the National Assembly.

Another pastor who entered politics to promote social reform was Friedrich von Bodelschwingh (1821–1910). In 1872 he accepted the directorship of the Rhenish-Westphalian home for epileptics and its deaconess home. Named Bethel, the center grew to include a training school for deacons, a theological school, and a home for destitute workers. Bodelschwingh's concern for the rehabilitation of the sick and the outcast led him to enter politics. Elected to the Prussian Diet in 1903, he secured passage of a law in 1907 that provided homes for itinerant workers. By this time the government began to favor such measures as means to undermine the socialist movement.

Bodelschwingh's son, of the same name (1877–1946), succeeded him as administrator of Bethel. The home was further enlarged, its medical facilities improved, and its research into the treatment of epilepsy expanded. At the beginning of the German church struggle against Hitler's effort to assimilate the church into the state, Bodelschwingh was elected national bishop, but the Nazi state nullified the election. He and his friends later led the opposition to the Nazi proposal to destroy all "life not worthy of living" and thereby protected the residents of Bethel and other institutions. Bethel continues to be a model of educational, therapeutic, and ecumenical diaconal work.

In spite of these and other exemplary efforts, evangelical social work in the nineteenth century remained a bourgeois concern; it gained little access to the industrial workers. The Inner Mission and diaconal movements were limited by their independence from the evangelical state churches, and by Protestant attachment to the government's opposition to socialism, communism, and democracy.

The response in America to comparable effects of industrialization and urbanization found voice and focus in the Social Gospel movement of the late nineteenth and early twentieth centuries. Washington Gladden (1836–1918), a Congregationalist minister, promoted the right of labor to organize. His many writings and hymns (e.g., "O Master, Let Me Walk with Thee") advocating Christian responsibility for social problems made him the "father" of the Social Gospel. The best known voice of the Social Gospel was the Baptist minister and professor Walter Rauschenbusch (1861–1918), whose *Christianity and the Social Crisis* (1907) gained international attention. He and his colleagues were oriented to a liberal Protestantism that stressed the realization of the Kingdom of God as the Christian goal. Their stress on social ethics modeled by Jesus is evident in the titles of some of Rauschenbusch's books (e.g., *Christianizing the Social Order* and *The Social Principles of Jesus*) as well as popular works directed toward the laity (e.g., William Stead's *If Christ Came to Chicago* and Charles Sheldon's immensely popular *In His Steps* – 25 million copies sold!). Rauschenbusch himself influenced progressive politics both at home and abroad; those who sought his advice included Theodore Roosevelt, Lloyd George, and Woodrow Wilson. However, World War I and then the Prohibition movement eroded the contributions of the Social Gospel.

The Catholic Church in the Nineteenth Century

After Napoleon's downfall, the Bourbons were restored to the French throne, and the papal states were restored to pope Pius VII. Conservatives presupposed that only a church supported by political authority could motivate and maintain the social bonds of society, and this stimulated a yearning for a unified Christian culture. The early Romantic movement transfigured the Middle Ages into such a culture. English Romanticism expressed the same fervor for Anglicanism as their French and German contemporaries did for Catholicism. A growing Catholic consciousness believed that only a strengthened papacy could renew the Catholic Church and thereby Western civilization.

Pius VII returned to Rome in 1814 after the abdication of Napoleon. The papacy regained its political freedom, and the Curia promoted the universal church against all tendencies toward national churches. The centralization of power in the papacy in opposition to national churches is known as ultramontanism (*ultra montes* – "beyond the mountains"). The restoration of the Papal States – a major thorn in the flesh of Italian aspiration for the unification of Italy – provided temporal security to a previously embattled papacy. In 1814 the pope reinstated the Jesuit order, whose influence continually increased in the course of the nineteenth century. The Jesuit ultramontanist offensive, abetted by an active Catholic press, expressed the anti-modernist spirit through revivals of medieval piety such as devotion to the Eucharist, the Sacred Heart, and Mary.

Pope Pius IX and Vatican I

Pius IX (r. 1846–78) focused the struggle against modernism. In 1854 he declared the first significant Marian dogma of the modern period: the Immaculate Conception of Mary. The dogma stated that Mary from the moment of her conception was free from all taint of original sin through a miraculous act of the Holy Spirit. Although a subject of medieval argument, this Marian dogma was proclaimed by Pius IX without consulting a council. The power of the pope to define dogma was a *fait accompli* even before it was justified by the dogma of papal infallibility.

In 1864 the "Syllabus of Errors" condemned rationalism, socialism, communism, Bible societies, and state independence in cultural and educational matters. Ultramontanist Catholicism rejected the separation of church and state, religious liberty, and public education without clerical control; and asserted the authority of the Catholic hierarchy to regulate public affairs. Civil legislation of marriage and divorce was not valid unless in conformity to canon law. The Catholic Church had the right to its own courts and police powers. The lasting impact of this upon the public imagination is exemplified by the specter of papal power raised during the election campaign of the American Catholic John F. Kennedy in 1960.

These developments culminated in the first Vatican Council (1869–70), which defined papal infallibility. The pope is infallible when he speaks "ex cathedra," that is, in the exercise of his teaching office on questions of faith and morals. Such infallible decisions must be made for the whole church and the foundation of faith "preserved holy and interpreted truly." Infallibility in doctrinal decisions was based in the papal decision not in the agreement of the church. Roman Catholicism became an absolute monarchy without constitutional restraints.

From Kulturkampf *to the Anti-Modernist Oath*

In general, the *Kulturkampf* refers to the clash of the Catholic Church with the spirit of liberalism and nationalism in the nineteenth century. In the narrower sense it was the struggle between the Prussian prime minister and chancellor Otto von Bismarck (1815–98) and the Roman Curia.

Bismarck wanted the churches, including the Protestant churches, out of state and political matters, and to confine them strictly to religious matters. Anti-Catholic legislation (1871–5) prohibited use of the pulpit for political agitation, expelled the Jesuits and related orders, and created state supervision of education. The so-called May Laws (1873) limited the disciplinary power of the church, instituted a Supreme Ecclesiastical Court, and mandated state control of all seminaries, including a state examination for all clergy. Pius IX condemned these laws in 1875 as subversive of the rights of the Church. Bismarck under-estimated the strength of Catholic and Protestant opposition to these laws, and since he also desired Catholic support in his opposition to social democracy, he gradually reversed his policy.

Pope Leo XIII (r. 1878–1903) eased tensions with his encyclical *Rerum Novarum*, the so-called "Magna Carta" of Catholic social teaching. It began with a strong defense of private property and condemned socialism and anarchism, but it also endorsed the grievances of the working class against their employers. Leo laid the blame for the intolerable inequities of capitalism and the industrial age at the feet of the powerful and the rich. The state is to be responsible for the common good; no class is to be exploited for the advantage of another; and there should be appropriate state actions to alleviate child labor and excessive working hours. Workers should receive a just wage to support their families. Leo's application of "Christian principles" to capital –labor relations won him the title "the working man's pope."

Leo maintained many of Pius IX's antagonisms toward the modern world. Since the end of the nineteenth century, reform-minded Catholics had fought against reactionary curialism for greater freedom in theology. Pius X (1903–14) condemned these efforts as "modernism," and all Catholic theologians had to take the so-called "anti-modernist oath" (1910, abrogated in 1967) before receiving a church office.

Nineteenth-Century Theology

Nineteenth-century German evangelical theology was particu-larly rich and pluralistic. Variations of Orthodoxy, Pietism, and the Enlightenment continued to exert influence, but in com-petition with new developments such as "liberalism" and "culture-Protestantism." The towering figure of these developments was Friedrich Daniel Ernst Schleiermacher (1768–1834). His many theological works included his early apologetic masterpiece *On Religion: Speeches to its Cultured Despisers* and a comprehensive dogmatics, *The Christian Faith*, that ranks with Calvin's *Institutes*. His modern critic Karl Barth wrote: "The first place in a history of theology of the most recent times belongs and will always belong to Schleiermacher, and he has no rival."

Schleiermacher took seriously the Enlightenment critiques of religion in general and Christianity in particular. He was convinced that faith loses its life when it tries to protect itself through self-defensive strategies. Thus he prefaced his dogmatics with Anselm's famous lines: "Nor do I seek to understand, in order that I may believe, but I believe, in order that I may understand. For he who does not believe, does not experience, and he who does not experience, does not understand." For Schleiermacher, the Christian community had to express its faith as clearly as possible in its particular context.

The Enlightenment and its development in Idealism stressed human freedom and autonomy. In conjunction with the natural sciences, the philosophers' turn to empirical experience reduced talk about the supernatural to the natural. Schleiermacher met this challenge on its own ground. He too began with experience; but in contrast to his age's infatuation with freedom, he spoke of human dependence. The experience of God is not dependent upon either intellectual abstractions or compulsions to believe unbelievable things, but rather is rooted in human experience itself as dependent experience. Hence his famous description of faith as "the consciousness of being absolutely dependent, or, which is the same thing, of being in relation to God." The Christian faith is not believing certain doctrines, living a certain way, or having heart-warming experiences, but rather living in relationship with God. That relationship focuses on Jesus of Nazareth as the mediator of faith that becomes real in the fellowship of believers, the church.

The Awakening

The "Awakening Movements" were, like Pietism, transconfessional religious upheavals beginning in England and North America and moving to the European continent. Their common marks included opposition to the Enlightenment; the seriousness of human sin before God; the new life dependent only on the grace of Christ; individual personal experience of rebirth; the rebirth of the individual leading to the restructuring of society; increased social activity and missionary efforts to spread the Christian faith.

The Awakenings spread through preaching, revivals, camp meetings, tract literature, and Bible and mission societies. The many waves of Awakening in England and North America were about a century earlier than in Germany. The rigorous New England Calvinism of the First Great Awakening epitomized by Jonathan Edwards' (1703–58) sermon "Sinners in the Hands of an Angry God" (1741) gave way to a more Arminian theology in the later revivals of the Second Great Awakening at the end of the eighteenth century. The latter sense of personal initiation of the process of salvation carried over into the evangelical abolitionist, temperance, and suffragist-feminist movements. The English Awakening reached its high point in the rise of the Methodist movement founded by the Anglican clergyman John Wesley (1703–91), whose efforts to renew spiritual life among the people were supported by his hymn-writing brother Charles Wesley (1707–88) and the evangelist George Whitfield (1714–70).

Methodist preaching spread revival throughout England, Scotland, Ireland, and North America. It called for personal discipleship to Christ; aimed at conversion under penitential struggle and the experience of grace; and led to strong communal expressions. Wesley's lay preaching office is characteristic for the Methodist movement. After Wesley's death, Methodism separated from the Anglican state church.

The Oxford Movement (1833–45) in the Anglican Church responded to the decline in church life, the spread of "liberalism" in theology, growing interest in the early and medieval church stimulated by Romanticism, and anxiety that the Catholic Emancipation Act (1829) would facilitate conversions to Roman Catholicism. The Oxford Movement's defense of the Church of England as a divine institution, the doctrine of apostolic succession, and the Book of Common Prayer as a rule of faith have played important roles in Anglican theology and ecclesiology up to today.

The concerns of the Oxford Movement were expressed through its *Tracts for the Times*, of which one of the most famous authors was John Henry Newman (1801–90). His *Tract No. 90* (1841) caused a major controversy by interpreting the Thirty-nine Articles, the Reformation platform for the Church of England, in congruity with the decrees of the Roman Catholic Council of Trent. A few years later Newman was received into the Catholic Church, and in 1879 was made a cardinal by pope Leo XIII. Newman's life and writings have been very influential on both the Church of England and the restoration of Catholicism in England and elsewhere.

Theological Currents

The optimism of the nineteenth century that "man" (!) is the "captain of his ship" and "master of his destiny" – a hubris only slightly dampened by the sinking of the *Titanic* in 1912 – was shared by the major theological currents of the nineteenth century.

Georg Wilhelm Friedrich Hegel (1770–1831), the epitome of German Idealism, culminated an era of supreme confidence in human rational thought. He posited the dialectical nature of reality in which everything is taken up in its opposition: thesis, antithesis, synthesis. The synthesis itself becomes a new thesis that is opposed and transcended into a new synthesis, and on and on; reality is a historical process in which the Absolute ("God" for the theologians) comes to its self-realization in our (i.e., Hegel's) reason. History is read as a dialectical process, an evolution moving toward fulfillment. Boarding the train of history is to participate in its goal, whether it be the Prussian state, the classless society, or any number of ideas Hegel's students promulgated.

History then is an intelligible order: "Everything real is rational and everything rational is real." This may not be much comfort to those who suffer the antitheses of history, but life must "suffer wounds" to be reconciled to its unity, and that the Spirit may come to self-realization through the process of estrangement and reconciliation. The appeal to theologians was the application of this system to the biblical views of God's purposes in history, the problem of theodicy, and the overcoming of the modern gulf between reason and revelation.

Hegel's more interesting students turned him on his head by asserting that materialism not idealism is the locus of reality. Hence, Feuerbach's concise statement: "One is what one eats." Marx, Engels, and Lenin developed Hegel's ideas into dialectical materialism and applied it to society and politics with the motto that our task is not to understand history but to change it. And Søren Kierkegaard (1813–55), the "father of existentialism," vehemently rejected Hegel's system altogether for the sake of the solitary individual who stands before the infinitely qualitative Other, God.

Feuerbach and Strauss, the *enfants terribles* of theology, were not shy about expressing their views of the old guard. Strauss said of one of his professors that if Jesus Christ had studied theology with him, he would have abandoned Christianity before he ever started it. Feuerbach, who influenced such figures as Marx, Friedrich Nietzsche, Sigmund Freud, and Martin Buber, has been called the "grave-digger of theology" who killed God and divinized humankind. Feuerbach caused all this excitement by interpreting Christianity as the projection of human fears and hopes. In his *Essence of Christianity* he wrote: "The personality of God is nothing else than the projected personality of man" and "the beginning, middle, and end of religion is MAN." Having gained his contemporaries' attention, Feuerbach went on to assert that to negate the subject (God) does not mean to negate the predicates (wisdom, love, justice). The real atheist, he said, is the person who theoretically acknowledges God and then lives as if God did not exist.

Strauss also unleashed a storm of controversy with his *Life of Jesus*, which argued that the Christ figure of the Gospel accounts is not historical but mythological. This was a terribly cold bath to the contemporary quest for the historical Jesus that posited an end run around critiques of Christian doctrine by historical research. For Strauss, Jesus was a teacher of love to God and the neighbor, and the idea of the God-man was attached to the figure of Jesus by the church.

The neuralgic issue of the relationship of faith and history, so sharply put by Strauss, was addressed by a theologian who credited his conversion to the Awakening, Martin Kähler (1835–1912). In his *The So-Called Historical Jesus and the Historic Biblical Christ* Kähler argued that the foundation of the Christian faith is not the historical Jesus but rather the Christ preached by the community. The attempt to draw a picture of the historical Jesus is an error because the Gospels are sources of the church's preaching rather than historical sources for the biography of Jesus. Kähler argued that the Christian community does not focus on the departed Jesus, but on the present living Christ; and that the certainty of faith cannot rest upon the results of historical scholarship.

Liberal Theology

Kähler's effort to disentangle faith from historical-empirical research did not resolve the problem of faith in relation to science and history for everyone. How is Christianity possible when the telescope, microscope, and stethoscope found no evidence of God "in the starry skies above and the moral law within"? The liberal answer posited trust in God on the encounter with Jesus. But lacking home videos by Mary and Joseph, how do we know who Jesus was and what he said? The response was to claim that Jesus was accessible through historical research. Hence the promotion of historical study of the New Testament and its environment to find the "real" Jesus behind the accretions of centuries of dogmatic developments.

Among the many major influential figures in liberal theology, Adolf von Harnack (1851–1930) and Ernst Troeltsch (1865–1923) deserve special mention. Harnack, a scholar of the ancient church and the history of dogma, strove to set forth a non-dogmatic Christianity peeled clean of the doctrinal layers added through history. The development of doctrine, Harnack argued, shifted the religion *of* Jesus (his proclamation of the Kingdom of God's love) to a religion *about* Jesus (a preexistent divine being who vicariously atoned for sin). He attributed the conception and development of dogma as "a work of the Greek spirit on the soil of the Gospel." Harnack proposed then to distinguish the kernel of the gospel from the husk of Greek philosophy.

The "kernel–husk" theory of the development of the Christian faith found expression in numerous nineteenth-century searches for the "essence" of Christianity. Harnack's own expression of this quest, *What is Christianity?*, reduced faith to the fatherhood of God, the brotherhood of humankind, and the infinite worth of the human soul. Received as a liberation from an outmoded faith and a key for salvaging Christianity for the modern world, the book went through 14 editions and as many translations by 1927. Nevertheless, these efforts to bring biblical proclamation into the present became increasingly problematic as the foreignness of the biblical message in contrast to modern conceptions became clear.

The problem of the relationship of faith and history was reflected above all in the work of Troeltsch, whose impact continues into the present. He focused on the relationships of Christianity to modern culture, revelation to history, and personal freedom to social conditions. Troeltsch's major legacy is his vigorous historicizing of all thinking. Nothing lies outside historical conditioning. The liberal hope of finding the "kernel," the "essence of Christianity," became as suspect as the conservative claim of the absoluteness of dogma. There is no non-historical, eternal kernel under the husk; everything exists in historical conditions. Relativism had reared its head. Troeltsch's *The Absoluteness of Christianity* made it clear that historical work as such cannot claim the superiority of one religion over another. Troeltsch realized that the historical method is a new wine that when introduced to the old wineskins of biblical studies, church history, and theology will burst them apart. But at this very point, European civilization itself burst apart, as it descended into the unprecedented mutual slaughter of World War I.

Chapter 11

The Christian Churches since World War I

World War I convulsed all areas of life. The breakdown of social and national order, the raging hatred among "civilized" nations of Europe, and the mass death upon the battlefields revealed the depths to which humankind can sink. The liberal optimism that had the temerity to think that this was the war to end all wars evaporated before the horrors of trench warfare and gas attacks. The "fatherhood of God, the brotherhood of humankind, and the infinite worth of the human soul" lost credibility as the "essence" of Christianity in view of the war between "Christian" nations.

The war's end did little to alleviate the nightmares of human-kind's dark side, for it created conditions favorable to the rise of Hitler and World War II. Psychologically unable to acknowledge defeat and misled by their leaders about the realities of the Versailles Peace Treaty, the German population reacted against the onerous terms of reparations and the "war-guilt" clause that demanded Germany accept sole responsibility for the war. A German nationalist reaction, coupled with nostalgia for the monarchy and a proud Prussian military history, fueled widespread anti-democratic bias against the new Weimar Republic (1919–33) and set the stage for Adolf Hitler.

The churches did little to stem raging nationalism. Before the war, many pastors and theologians had actively fostered nationalism. Now they preached against the "war-guilt lie" and looked to a future divine vindication of the nation and the abolition of the Treaty of Versailles. As National Socialism appeared on the scene the danger of its ideology was not widely perceived.

The interwar years were in some respects not as difficult for the Catholic Church as for the Protestant ones. The end of the German monarchy left Catholicism undisturbed in its life under the pope. Furthermore, the Catholic Center Party, next to the Social Democrats one of the essential supporters of the new Weimar Republic, represented Catholic interests in opposition to the pretensions of Prussian Protestantism. Also, in the 1920s, Catholicism experienced fruitful developments in monastic and liturgical renewal.

New Formulations in Protestant Theology

In Germany the idealistic enthusiasm at the beginning of World War I awakened hopes of religious renewal. But the churches, filled in the first year of the war, were soon once again empty. The expectation that materialism and socialism would be overcome, and that people – especially the worker class – would return to the churches was disappointed. The "dechristianization" begun in the nineteenth century became "dechurchification" as the war promoted rather than halted alienation from the church. All too frequently after the war the pastors found themselves preaching to the choir of the conservative middle class and civil servants mourning the lost monarchy.

However, some voices began to pose striking alternatives to the contemporary throne and altar ideology of a synthesis of

Christianity and culture. Rudolf Otto's (1869–1937) *The Idea of the Holy* presented God not as the extension of humankind, but as the "totally other." The same year, Karl Holl's (1866–1926) *What did Luther Understand by Religion?* displaced liberal images of Luther as the hero and fighter for national liberty by presenting Luther's theology of sin, evil, and justification through the cross and suffering. Holl's work initiated the so-called Luther renaissance that also had great significance for the development of dialectical theology. A factor in the impact of this research was the theological and pastoral question of whether any other period in history had faced comparable religious and social crises.

The most important theological reorientation after World War I was the dialectical theology closely tied to Karl Barth. Barth, one of Harnack's prize students, became a pastor in 1911 in Safenwill, a worker community in his native Switzerland. Here Barth soon discovered that his vaunted education in liberalism had not prepared him for ministry in the context of the socio-economic problems of his parish. Shocked by the low wages of the workers and disturbed that his wealthy parishioners saw no conflict between exploitation and the Christian faith, Barth became radicalized personally, politically, and theologically. He became a social democrat, that is, in his context a Marxist without communism, and earned the nickname "the red pastor." Required to preach, he discovered the Bible a "strange new world" rather than the blueprint for liberalism's great society. The next shock for Barth came with the outbreak of World War I when he saw, to his horror, that many of his learned professors signed the "Declaration of German Intellectuals" in support of "emperor and fatherland." It was now clear to him that liberalism was politically, socially, ethically, and religiously bankrupt.

Together with his friend and fellow-pastor Eduard Thurneysen (1888–1974), who mediated to him the writings of the Russian Orthodox novelist Fyodor Dostoyevski (1821–81), Barth turned his back on liberal theology and sought answers to his questions in the Bible. It is said that his *Commentary on Romans* (1918, second, reworked edition 1922) "fell like a bombshell on the playground of the theologians." Here the Bible is the address of the transcendent God who reveals himself in his judgment of the world in the death and resurrection of Christ. In this light all religion, including Christianity, is a human enterprise under God's judgment. Here, too, Barth echoed that great Dane, Søren Kierkegaard (1813–55), whose attack on both Hegel and bourgeois Christendom emphasized the "infinite qualitative difference" between God and humankind.

Barth and Thurneysen were soon joined by others: the Swiss Reformed theologian Emil Brunner (1889–1966), who blamed Schleiermacher for the misery of theology; the German Lutheran theologians Friedrich Gogarten (1887–1969), who came to similar insights through study of Luther, and Rudolf Bultmann (1884–1976), whose avenue to dialectical theology was through New Testament research and the rediscovery of Reformation theology. The German Lutheran theologian Paul Tillich (1886–1965) shared some of their concerns but was forced as a Religious Socialist to leave Germany in 1933; he then became a major theological voice in America. The movement of dialectical theology – shorthand for God's "no" to the world and sin which contained his "yes" of redemption – effectively spread its views through its own theological journal *Zwischen den Zeiten* (Between the Times) that lasted from 1923 to 1933.

Barth himself moved on to a series of German professorships until deported for criticism of the Nazis. At Bonn, Barth informed his students it would be in bad taste to begin a lecture on the Sermon on the Mount with "Heil Hitler." More forceful criticisms of National Socialism brought Barth before a Nazi court on the charge of seducing the minds of his students. His defense was to read Socrates' defense before the court of Athens. The judges were not amused, and Barth was expelled. He then became a professor at Basel.

The Churches during National Socialism

In 1933 Adolf Hitler and his National Socialist Party seized power. The Party program asserted its support for "positive Christianity," by which it meant churches in service to the state. But few at the time had any sense of Hitler's intention to replace the Christian faith with his own brand of brutal paganism of "blood and soil." In fact, during the 12 years of National Socialist rule only the first steps were enacted, mainly the co-option of the churches by state supervision and deconfessionalization. The "final solution" for the churches was to be completed after the war.

Nazi inroads into the churches were facilitated both by the churches' false sense of security concerning Nazi intentions, and by the enthusiastic reception of Hitler not only by many church members but also by many pastors. Before Hitler came to power, Catholic bishops warned of the dangers of National Socialism and forbade Catholics from joining the Party. Afterwards, however, the bishops muted their opposition. Catholics as well as Protestants were attracted to the new authoritarian regime by its rapid social accomplishments and suppression of communism. By the end of March 1933 the conference of German bishops declared their earlier warnings invalid. By the next July Hitler had removed potential problems with Catholicism by negotiating a Concordat with the Vatican. The regime promised to protect Catholic schools, institutions, and clergy in return for the cessation of all German Catholic political and social organizations. Soon, however, Nazi restrictions of the Catholic press, schools, and youth organizations created conflicts that were intensified by the church's condemnations of the paganism and totalitarian claims of National Socialism. In 1937 Pius XI's encyclical *Mit brennender Sorge* (With profound concern), strongly condemning National Socialism, was read from Catholic pulpits. Individual bishops and priests courageously opposed the Nazi programs to exterminate all Jews and all others deemed unworthy of life, such as the mentally and physically impaired. Consequently, numerous priests were imprisoned and murdered.

The Nazi program to domesticate the Protestant churches began with the proposal to unify the 28 "state" churches in a national Protestant Church. The churches' vulnerability to National Socialism related to the liberal theological heritage of "culture Protestantism" and the reactionary nationalist spirit following World War I that projected Germany's defeat upon evil foreign forces and internal atheistic subversion. Already in the 1920s there were voices scapegoating Jews and advocating purifying Christianity of its Jewish heritage. However, church authorities too frequently dismissed them as just the lunatic fringe of society.

The racist Protestants found a warm welcome in the National- ist Socialist Party. In the spring of 1932 the National Socialists advanced the "German Christian Faith Movement" that vigor- ously promoted a nationalistic racism including the removal of all Jewish influences. The German Christians aroused an amaz- ing response. People who had not darkened church doors in years now came out and darkened the church itself by electing German Christians to a third of the seats in the church govern- ment; by the summer of 1933 they were the majority.

The German Christians now openly attacked the churches. In order to safeguard the independence of the church, the evan- gelical state churches presented the highly respected Friedrich von Bodelschwingh as their own candidate for the office of Reichsbishof. Outside pressure and inner disunity led however to Bodelschwingh's resignation, and Hitler appointed an army chaplain, Ludwig Müller (1883–1945), national bishop. Supported by the full Nazi apparatus of press and radio propaganda, the German Christians proceeded to Nazify the church. Using the Civil Service Law (1933) that mandated the removal of all non- Aryan (that is, Jewish) officials from every level of government, the German Christians removed all clergy of Jewish descent and also all opponents of the Nazis.

The German Christians' effort to insert the non-Aryan para-graph into the constitution of the church precipitated the *Kirchenkampf* (church struggle). The World War I submarine hero and now pastor, Martin Niemöller (1892–1986), led the opposi-tion. He founded the "Pastors' Emergency League," followed by "Councils of the Brethren," as alternative church authorities wherever the official church was ruled by the German Christians. These groups gained support from leading members of the theo-logical faculties, including the not-yet expelled Karl Barth and the younger pastor Dietrich Bonhoeffer (1906–45), who was later executed for participating in the abortive plot to assassinate Hitler. Many of these pastors were later disposed of by conscripting them into the army, where they lost their lives. However, their revivifying of theology and their witness remained influential.

In May 1934 these pastors formed the "Confessing Church." Their Barmen Declaration rejected any and all synthesis of Chris-tian faith and National Socialism, and proclaimed exclusive alle-giance to the claims of biblical revelation. The authors made clear that if the German Christians succeeded, the church would cease to be the church. The Barmen Declaration thus witnessed to the importance of memory and history for the identity of the church and its confession. Barth, a major drafter of the Barmen Declaration, later regretted he had not made solidarity with the Jews a decisive feature of the text.

The one who made it crystal clear that racism denies the gospel was Dietrich Bonhoeffer, himself influenced by Barth. Bonhoeffer's essay "The Church and the Jewish Question" pub-licly stated that the Christian community is called "not just to bandage the victims under the wheel, but to put a spoke in the wheel itself. Such action would be direct political action." It is of interest that a couple of years before this Bonhoeffer had spent a year studying theology in New York City, and American racism had profoundly disturbed him.

In spite of persecution the clergy and laity of the Confessing Church continued to oppose the National Socialist regime until the outbreak of the war in 1939 ended public resistance. In this period conflicts within the Confessing Church over theological issues, above all the question of what makes the church the church, led Bonhoeffer to declare in 1936: "Whoever knowingly separates himself from the Confessing Church in Germany, separates himself from salvation."

The Confessing Church was also influential in Nazi-occupied territories such as the Netherlands, Norway, and France. As a European movement the Confessing Church contributed to the nascent ecumenical movement that blossomed after the war. The Barmen Confession remains a model statement of faith in areas of church–state confrontation and political oppression. It influenced the *Kairos* document (1985), a theological watershed of opposition to apartheid in South Africa, and the world confessional bodies of the World Alliance of Reformed Churches and the Lutheran World Federation in their condemnations of apartheid. The latter's position that apartheid ("apartness" – the South African National Party's platform of racial segregation to maintain white dominance) constitutes a confessional issue echoed Bonhoeffer's statement in 1938 that where the church is "subjected by outside force to a law which is alien to the church it may not yield, but must bear witness in word and deed to its freedom from the alien law and its sole obedience to Jesus Christ." When the integrity of the church is threatened, nothing is indifferent.

Bonhoeffer himself had ample opportunity for safety in a pastorate in London and offers of professorships in America, but was committed to serving his people in the Confessing Church. In *The Cost of Discipleship* he wrote: "When Christ calls a man, he bids him come and die." His emphasis upon "costly grace" critiqued what he called the "cheap grace" of all syntheses of Christ and culture. His emphasis "that a church without a confession is a church lost and defenseless, and that it is in its confession that a church has the only weapon that will not break," continues to be relevant to contemporary churches and the ecumenical movement.

National Socialism forced the Confessing Church underground. Niemöller, imprisoned at the Dachau concentration camp from 1938 to 1945, and Bonhoeffer, imprisoned in 1943 and executed in 1945, were among countless others, clergy and laity, Protestant and Catholic, who paid dearly to confess their faith. In the face of the Nazi pogrom against the Jews there were heroic actions by individual Christians, but there was no concerted public intervention. Immediately after the war, the Council of the German Protestant Churches acknowledged this in the "Stuttgart Declaration of Guilt" (October 1945) presented to the representatives of the Ecumenical Council of Churches: "We have for many years fought in the name of Jesus Christ against the spirit which in the name of National Socialism found terrifying expression; but we indict ourselves that we did not more courageously confess, more faithfully pray, more joyously believe, and more passionately love."

Developments in the Catholic Church after World War I

The pontificate of Pius XI (1922–39) was especially significant in directing the Catholic Church in opposing modern liberalism. He concluded many concordats, including that with Hitler in 1933. In 1929 the Lateran Treaty ended the long papal conflict with the Italian state and established the full sovereignty of the Vatican City. Among Pius XI's encyclicals were *Casti connubi* (1930) that condemned contraception and sought respect for married life, and *Quadragesimo Anno* (1931) that confirmed and elaborated the points of Leo XIII's *Rerum Novarum*, stressing the evils of both free capitalism and strict socialism. Pius XI was also called the "Pope of Catholic Action." Through activation of the laity under clerical leadership all social life should be filled with

Catholic impulses. Catholic Action testified to a self-conscious, powerfully active Catholicism after the war.

The activation of the laity was particularly evident in the religious renewal of youth. Catholic student and worker associations further promoted the mobilization of the laity. The living piety of modern Catholicism found expression in the renewal of monastic life, and in biblical and liturgical movements. In 1933 the Catholic Bible Work was founded to promote understanding of the Bible; and the Una Sancta movement continued this orientation while promoting understanding of other churches and seeking to soften the positions of the Counter-Reformation. The liturgical movement desired to move from modern subjectivism back to the treasures of the ancient church, including Gregorian chant and emphasis upon the communal character of the mass. Its main centers were the Benedictine cloisters of Beuron and Maria Laach, and it was closely tied to the Catholic youth movement.

Pius XII (r. 1939–58) remains controversial for dealing with National Socialism through traditional diplomacy, and for not publicly addressing the Nazi persecution of the Jews. He did continue his predecessors' condemnation of communism, and issued a blanket excommunication of members of communist parties and organizations. His more liberal tendencies supported the liturgical movement and biblical studies. *Divino afflante spiritu* (1943) allowed more liberty for scientific biblical study, and limited the normative character of the Vulgate Bible to the liturgy.

On the other hand, Pius XII condemned once again modernist theological movements, especially the "new theology" in France, in his *Humani generis* (1950). More noteworthy is the dogmatizing of the assumption of Mary in Pius XII's bull *Munificentissimus Deus* (1950). It concluded the development of Marian dogma since 1854, and underscored the great significance of Mariology in modern Catholicism. It was also the first use of the dogma of papal infallibility since Vatican I.

The most outstanding event in twentieth-century Catholicism is certainly the Second Vatican Council (1962–5). The largest council in church history, it began under pope John XXIII (r. 1958–63) and concluded under Paul VI (r. 1963–78). The council's achievements included renovation of the image of the church as "the people of God," a community of faith, sacrifice, prayer, and love; renewal of the liturgy by introduction of vernacular languages instead of mandatory Latin in worship; greater participation of the congregation, including allowing the cup to the laity at communion; strengthening the office of the bishop and the college of bishops so that in communion with the pope the bishops work together in leading the church, and presenting the papal office as service rather than rule; and the promotion of ecumenism and the desire for community with separated Christians.

The Ecumenical Movement

Rebuilding the European churches after World War II was closely connected to the most significant church historical event of the twentieth century, the ecumenical movement. It too had its roots in the nineteenth century through the cooperative work of the churches in mission fields and diaconal work. Although the Roman Catholic Church is not a member of the World Council of Churches, the relationships between the Catholic Church and the Protestant churches markedly improved in the late twentieth century.

Well before the first assembly of the World Council of Churches in Amsterdam in 1948, there had been proposals for an international Christian association. Joseph Oldham (1874–1969) had suggested to a meeting of mission leaders in 1920 that the coordination of Christian mission would probably have to develop into something like a world league of churches. Oldham, one of the chief architects of the ecumenical movement, was born in

Bombay, and planned to enter the Indian civil service after his education in Edinburgh and Oxford. A conversion experience at an Oxford meeting led by the American evangelist Dwight L. Moody radically altered his plans. Remaining a layman, he was active in the missionary struggle against racism in colonial Africa and he strove to assist the church in addressing the modern world.

Throughout the early history of the ecumenical movement lay leadership played an important role. One of Oldham's significant lay colleagues was the American Methodist John R. Mott (1865–1955). Converted while a student at Cornell, he was traveling secretary of the YMCA, and in 1895 participated in the founding meeting in Sweden of the World Student Christian Federation. Mott, like many of his contemporaries, saw students as the lever by which the world would be moved toward God. With his friend Nathan Söderblom, Mott saw the value of international Christian witness to issues of peace and justice. His many efforts in this direction led to the award of the Nobel Peace Prize in 1946.

Calls for ecumenical organization – including an encyclical letter in 1920 by the Ecumenical Patriarch of Constantinople – reflected the late nineteenth-century missionary activities and evangelical revivals in Europe and North America. In the 1890s the Student Volunteer Movement for Foreign Missions issued an urgent call to "evangelize the world in this generation." The tensions and divisions of confessional identities transplanted from Europe to America and to the mission fields had hampered such zeal, and were therefore addressed at the World Missionary Conference in Edinburgh (1910).

The delegates to the Edinburgh conference, mainly North Americans and Europeans, were from Protestant mission societies, not from the churches. But even with these limitations, the Edinburgh conference has been described as "one of the great landmarks in the history of the church" and the birthplace of the ecumenical movement. It was this meeting that led to the formation of the International Missionary Council, instrumental in forming local and national structures of ecumenism.

Charles Brent, an American Episcopalian and later bishop of the Philippines, and one of the missionaries at Edinburgh, was convinced that the divisive issues of doctrine and church order – deliberately not treated at Edinburgh – were crucial issues for the future of the churches. After years of labor and the intervention of World War I, his vision was realized at the 1927 World Conference on Faith and Order. Some 400 delegates, from over a hundred churches, met in Lausanne.

Two years earlier, in 1925, the Universal Christian Conference on Life and Work had met in Stockholm and encouraged the churches cooperatively to address social issues. All the delegates were official representatives of their own churches, and there was a strong Eastern Orthodox presence. The central figure was Nathan Söderblom (1866–1931), the archbishop of Stockholm, a historian of religions and a pioneer in bringing Orthodox and evangelical churches together. In 1930 he was awarded the Nobel Peace Prize for his initiatives for common Christian responsibility in international peace, freedom, and justice.

Some of the delegates at Lausanne were concerned that the Stockholm emphasis on "applied Christianity" would give precedence to interchurch collaboration on social issues over the search for church unity. The tension between these two concerns continued for many years, but the Life and Work movement itself began to realize that its slogan "doctrine divides and service unites" could not gloss over different theological understandings of the Kingdom of God. The growing tension over this issue led to a plan to merge Life and Work with Faith and Order. A 1938 conference in Utrecht made plans for a 1941 inaugural assembly of a World Council of Churches to incorporate this concern, but it had to be put on hold due to the outbreak of World War II.

At Utrecht, Willem A. Visser 't Hooft (1900–85) was invited to become general secretary of the World Council of Churches "in process of formation," a post he held until retirement in

1966. Visser 't Hooft had experienced ecumenism in the Student Christian Movement. After his theological studies he joined the Geneva staff of the YMCA. In this position he became involved with Christians from many churches, and then met John R. Mott. Visser 't Hooft expressed his unwavering commitment to church unity in his observation that Christ did not pray "that they may all enter into conversation with one another; he prayed that they all may be one."

The first assembly of the World Council of Churches (WCC) was held in Amsterdam in 1948. Its theme, "Man's Disorder and God's Design," reflected the disasters of World War II and acknowledged that the recent horrors testified in part to the churches' failures. The concern for international order reflected not only the recent past but also the steadily worsening relations between East and West. Hence the famous exchange between the American Presbyterian delegate John Foster Dulles, later the United States' Secretary of State, and the Czech theologian Josef Hromádka.

Dulles described communism as the greatest obstacle to world peace. Hromádka pleaded for a sympathetic understanding of communism as a force embodying much of the social impetus that the church and Western civilization should have been representing. In response to their sharp exchange, the assembly insisted that no civilization can escape the radical judgment of the Word of God, and explicitly rejected the assumption that capitalism and communism were the only available choices.

Future controversies were foreshadowed in the assembly's rejection in principle of war "as contrary to the will of God," while at the same time recognizing that this position was not accepted unanimously throughout Christendom. The assembly also stated that every kind of tyranny and imperialism calls for opposition and struggle to secure human rights and basic liberties. Ecumenical efforts to put these words into practice elicited strong reactions. In the 1980s both *Reader's Digest* and the *Sixty Minutes* television program claimed the WCC and the US National Council of Churches were supporting revolutionary and Marxist causes with money given by Christians. On the other hand, communist regimes attacked the WCC for its stand on human rights. The WCC's efforts for peace in the Middle East and the dismantling of apartheid also created what one observer called the "ecumenical character-assassination game." Conservative theological critics, reflecting the early twentieth-century fundamentalist–modernist conflict, have accused the WCC of being an exponent of "liberal theology."

The years following Amsterdam focused on responding to the vast human needs created by the war. Programs of interchurch aid, service to refugees and international affairs, loan funds, and reconstruction were major expressions of ecumenical life and work. The churches through the WCC would have to show, Visser 't Hooft stated, that their coming together "made a real difference."

In this light, the second assembly of the WCC (Evanston, 1954) met with the theme, "Christ – the Hope of the World." The assembly discussion became stormy as it became apparent that talk about hope raised a central theological issue: how does the Christian's hope for the coming of God's Kingdom relate to hopes for immediate improvements in people's lives? Those who emphasized the former tended to think of those who emphasized the latter as superficial optimists and activists, who in turn charged them with being out of touch with the "real world." The assembly itself could not agree on a formulation of how Christian hope here and now is related to ultimate hope. Nevertheless, priority was given to the problems of undeveloped regions, the arms race, and racism. The omnipresence of the Cold War was seen not only in these issues but also in the addresses by such public figures as US president Eisenhower and UN secretary general Dag Hammskjöld.

The WCC was slow to grasp the urgency of the socioeconomic problems facing the so-called "Third World," and like the UN was divided over how fast and far the decolonization process should go. Asian churches at a 1952 meeting in Lucknow, India, sponsored by the WCC, explicitly linked the Cold War and accelerating movements for independence. They insisted that the challenge of communism could be best met by a positive attitude to the social revolution taking place in East Asia. The Lucknow conference called for radical reform of land tenure systems, planned economic development, and church support for struggles for freedom and self-determination. A few months later the WCC Central Committee took up this challenge and launched national, regional, and global conferences and publications to support churches facing "rapid social change."

Succeeding assemblies of the WCC dealt with expanding ecumenical relationships as well as social ethical concerns. The affirmation of the uniqueness of Christ – an echo of the early church's Arian controversy – raised the issue of the relationship of Christianity to other religions. And pope John XXIII's invitation to the WCC to send observers to the sessions of the Second Vatican Council facilitated far-reaching changes in Roman Catholic–Protestant relations. One of the persistent social issues, however, was racism. Martin Luther King, Jr. was to address the WCC assembly in Uppsala in 1968, but was assassinated four months before the meeting. James Baldwin reminded the assembly of the long history of church involvement in racial injustice, and asked whether "there is left in Christian civilization the moral energy, the spiritual daring, to atone, to repent, to be born again." While insisting that proclamation of the gospel is essential, the assembly also insisted that Christian worship is ethical and that any segregation by race or class must be rejected. Future assemblies were marked by renewed commitments to human rights and the struggles for justice.

It should be noted that at the same time that the WCC was developing and growing, world communions of churches such as the Lutheran World Federation, the World Alliance of Reformed Churches, and the World Methodist Council among others, had begun and now continue to be involved in bilateral and multilateral dialogues among each other and with other churches, such as the Roman Catholic and Pentecostal churches.

The striving for reunion of separated confessions is one of the most significant aspects of modern church history. Rooted in the period of Pietism, it extended into the nineteenth-century Awakenings, and provided impulses to transconfessional and supranational connections in social and missionary endeavors. The ecumenical movement's conferences in the twentieth century provided many incentives to the rapprochement of the Christian churches, and essentially changed the climate between the churches in comparison to prior centuries.

Back to the Future: Christianity in Global Context

Our narrative of the history of Christianity now verges on journalism as we try to picture contemporary developments. It may well be that the most significant development in the modern story of Christianity is its remarkable shift from "Eurocentric" denominationalism to a truly global movement whose center of gravity is now the southern hemisphere of Latin America, sub-Saharan Africa, and Asia, and whose form is increasingly a trans-denominational Protestantism. In contrast to the efforts by the modern Western churches to adapt the faith to modern culture, the younger churches bear a stronger resemblance to the early churches' belief in prophecy, faith healing, exorcism, visions, and charismatic leadership. Like the early church, the younger churches confronted by pluralism and its concomitant relativism have embraced Christian identity, albeit in inculturated forms. The variety of new forms of churches as "community churches" also has a certain parallel to the early church in their decentralization. The old saying that all politics is local may perhaps be paraphrased to say that many churches are developing from the local context rather than depending upon denominational missions.

This by no means gainsays the contributions of historical missions from Paul onward. Jesuit missions reached Asia in the sixteenth century, and Protestant missions from Halle and then the major nineteenth-century British and American mission endeavors extended to the four corners of the world. What is noteworthy in the present is that the perceived and often all too actual relations between Christian missions and European exploration and empire building began to recede with the process of decolonization. As former colonies have gained their independence from imperial powers, so too have the mission churches. The consequent inculturation and indigenization of the local churches – phenomena evident also in the early churches' mission – are contributing a remarkable vitality to the so-called "younger churches."

Whatever the trends of the present, the old saw that the more things change the more they stay the same may prompt reflection on the development of Christian identity in history. What has stayed the same for the "one, holy, catholic church, the communion of saints" is *anamnesis* – Jesus' mandate to live "in remembrance" of him.

Appendix

Periodization

The memory and identity of the Christian community as it is handed on has influenced the understanding of the history of Christianity and the periodization of history in general. Until recently the collectors and tellers of the family conversations of Christianity were nearly all insiders. Thus the subject matter and the discipline of telling the gospel story were under the rubric of "church history." In modern times, for a variety of reasons, persons outside the Christian churches are also interested in presenting the history of Christianity. There is, to paraphrase the old saw, the sense that the telling of the story of the Christian contributions to contemporary identity is too important to be left to the Christians.

Since the eighteenth-century Enlightenment, there has been suspicion that the story of Christianity as told by its historians has been influenced by partisan polemics presented as objective truth. Thus a brief discussion of the distinct perspectives of church historians and historians of Christianity may be useful in reading both contemporary textbooks and historical sources. Some of the presuppositions that govern an author's interpretation of events and texts leap right off the page at us; others are more subtle and difficult to recognize – especially if we share the worldview of the authors. An example of the former are the miracle stories which lace one of our important sources for early medieval English history, the eighth-century *History of the English Church and People* by Bede. The two early church historians most influential upon the conceptualizing of the history of Christianity are Eusebius, bishop of Caesarea (ca. 260–ca. 339) and Augustine, bishop of Hippo (354–430). Eusebius is known as the "father of church history" because his *The History of the Church from Christ to Constantine* is the first history of the church outside the Book of Acts in the New Testament. Eusebius, by the way, was quite up front about his method of constructing his narrative: "From the scattered hints dropped by my predecessors I have picked out whatever seems relevant to the task I have undertaken, plucking like flowers in literary pastures the helpful contributions of earlier writers to be embodied in the continuous narrative I have in mind." Eusebius lived through the persecutions that accompanied the transition from the pagan to the Christian empire. Thus it is not surprising that the emperor Constantine, in his view God's agent for the church, plays a central role in this and his other historical work, the *Chronicle*, and that the unity of church and empire is God's plan. The *Chronicle* found numerous imitators and influenced medieval conceptions of world history as guided by the providence of God, bracketed by the creation and the Last Judgment. The classic expression of this genre is Augustine's *The City of God*, which presents history in terms of the people of God as pilgrims in an alien world traveling to the heavenly city. Augustine's eschatological orientation, conceived in the context of the fall of Rome and dominated by his understanding of the Bible, remained the basic orientation of history in the West until the Enlightenment. In contrast to Hellenistic views of history as cyclical, a repetitive "wheel," the biblical view of history is that it is linear, beginning with God's creation and progressing to its divine fulfillment. The basis of history for Augustine is not fate or human activity but the unfolding of God's plan. Augustine thus presented a theology of history.

In *The Myth of Christian Beginnings* Robert Wilken states: "Historical thinking is and should be selective" and "Christians, like others, cultivate the memory of the past for the uses of the present." The question of course is why historians select what they do for their narratives. The choice of miracle stories or divinely guided emperors clearly intends to advance the story of the Christian church. We are not surprised that in such examples the presuppositions are theological. As you are well aware, there are also other presuppositions active in historical studies, such as gender, race, and culture, that may not be so evident. As scholars in our own day struggle to bring awareness of the historical roles of women in the church, or slavery, or the once-dominant Eurocentric view of Christianity, there is recognition that the nineteenth-century historians' ideal of presenting the "facts" "exactly as they happened" has been undermined by our awareness of the role of the "self-evident" in history. This means that the profoundest mark of any age is what it accepts as self-evident, as the basic assumptions that tend to be held by everyone, friend and foe alike. It is difficult to assess the self-evident because it constitutes the very air an age breathes. Thus, for a modern culture fascinated by the "self-evident" value of innovation, it is difficult to appreciate the Eusebian concern for origins in the sense that "older is better." Other examples: prior to the modern ecumenical movement, historians tended to assume that schism in the Western church was the norm, and thus viewed the Protestant–Catholic colloquies of the sixteenth century differently than they do now; or, because the later church was patriarchal, historians tended to assume that women did not play significant leadership roles in the early church.

Historians no less than theologians are tempted to identify "history" as the actuality of the past with "history" as the construction they create from its records. For history as the actuality of the past, an "age" is simply a considerable span of time. For history as construction of the past, an "age" is a segment of the past on which the historian imposes some intelligibility. For example, the construction of history on the basis of the idea of progress, or human control over the course of history, creates the poignant predicament of choosing which myth is most useful to impose dramatic organization upon the data. This is a problem that pre-Renaissance historians, unfettered by belief in human freedom, did not have.

But let us go back to Eusebius and his influence upon the writing of histories of Christianity up to the modern period. The norm for Eusebius' church is the community of the first two centuries of the Christian era. From his time on, Christians would rationalize historical change and development as faithful expressions of early Christianity, and would so idealize the apostolic time, the time of origins, that even today theological curricula frequently separate biblical and historical studies, thus echoing the old conviction that the Bible, as the record of origins, precedes historical development. A century after Eusebius, Vincent of Lérins (d. ca. 450) provided a famous formula for true Christianity. The so-called Vincentian canon states that "the true faith is that which has been believed everywhere, always, and by all." In other words, the true and authentic teachings of the church had remained and will remain the same from the very beginning of Christianity. This formula, by the way, provided a simple means of determining who is a heretic: anyone who breaks this unity of doctrine, that is, who deviates from the tried and true, and innovates.

The Eusebian model that older is better continued to be influential into the early modern Renaissance (fourteenth to sixteenth centuries). The Humanists spoke of the roughly thousand-year period from the end of the classical Roman era to their own time as the "Middle Ages." They considered the Middle Ages as an intermediate period between what they perceived as the ideal classical period and their own time. They viewed their recovery of ancient literature and classical languages (Hebrew, Greek, and Latin) as the rebirth (hence, "Renaissance") of education, science, art, and the church. Their motto was *ad fontes* – back to the sources.

While *ad fontes* remains a watchword for historians, the Humanists gave it a pejorative slant. They regarded the Middle Ages as barbaric; it was the "gothic" (i.e., barbaric) age. This characterization was driven not just by aesthetic–philological criteria, but also by theological and religious criteria. The men and women of the Renaissance projected back into history their own reaction to what they regarded as the bigoted and narrow-minded authoritarianism and orthodoxy of their day. Their influence is evident in the continued usage of labels for the Middle Ages such as "Dark Ages" and "scholastic." Such value judgments received sharper edges by the continuation of the Renaissance in the seventeenth and eighteenth-century Enlightenment attacks upon the clergy as ignorant and superstitious, as well as the Enlightenment ideal of autonomy from all external authorities, including the church.

Even though the Reformations of the sixteenth century fragmented the medieval church, all parties continued to hold the Eusebian model of church history by claiming to be *the* faithful recovery or continuation of the early church, and by accusing all the other churches of being innovators. The Reformers urged people to judge all doctrines by scripture. And all the churches turned to studies of history to bolster their individual claims to be *the* community faithful to the tradition. Those convinced that the medieval church was nothing less than a total corruption of the primitive church developed martyrologies to support their view that in spite of corruption there continued to be faithful witnesses to the Jesus movement in history. In short, selective memories were at work in all parties.

The first comprehensive Protestant church history elaborated in great detail the claim that there had always been persons who had opposed the innovations and errors of the papacy. Under the leadership of the Lutheran Matthew Flacius Illyricus (1520–75), a group of scholars developed a history of the church from its beginning down to 1400 titled *Historia Ecclesia Christi*. Since this work divided the history of the church into centuries and was begun in the city of Magdeburg, it came to be known as the "Magdeburg Centuries." The Eusebian model of historical periodization remained effective in Flacius' argument that the Reformation was the restoration of the original purity of the church. Not surprisingly for a Lutheran apologist, the key to the faithfulness of the church was seen to be the doctrine of justification by grace alone. The original purity of the church lasted to about 300, and with some reservations perhaps even up to 600, but then there had been a falling away from the true faith due to the expansion of papal authority.

Not to be outdone, the Roman Catholic Church responded to the Magdeburg Centuries with the herculean efforts of Caesar Baronius (1538–1607). After thirty years of work in the Vatican archives, Baronius began publishing his study of the history of the church. In contrast to the Protestant chronology of centuries, Baronius proceeded year by year. By the time of his death, his *Annales Ecclesiastici* had reached the year 1198. No less partisan than Flacius, and equally subject to the Eusebian model, Baronius focused his study on the institution of the papacy rather than on the doctrine of justification.

In terms of periodization, the Magdeburg Centuries set forth the three periods of history now familiar to us: the ancient church, or time of origins up to about 300; the medieval period of decay, about 300 to 1500; and the new or modern period of recovery. The historical reality of this tripartite division of ancient–medieval–modern was little questioned, and passed into the schema of universal history by the end of the seventeenth century through the *Historia tripartita* of Christoph Cellarius (Keller; 1634–1707).

Cellarius divided history by monarchies, employing a periodization that went back to the vision of four beasts in Daniel 7:1–8 and their interpretation in ancient Christian historiography as four world empires on the basis of Daniel 7:17–27. For Cellarius, ancient history extended to the Roman emperor Constantine (ca. 288–337), the medieval period extended to the end of the Byzantine Empire (1453), and modern history was synchronized with the Reformation and its aftermath.

In the late seventeenth century a new historical perspective came to the fore in church historical writing. This new interpretive principle for history displaced the doctrinal and institutional principles running from the works of Eusebius and Augustine through those of Flacius and Baronius by that of religious experience, that is, personal piety and life. The work that uniquely and forcefully advocated this interpretation of history was by the radical Pietist Gottfried Arnold (1666–1714). His *Impartial History of the Church and of Heretics from the Beginning of the New Testament to the Year of Christ 1688* was of course no less "impartial" than its predecessors. But it did introduce a new perspective that with variations on the theme remains in vogue: history from the perspective of the marginalized. To Arnold, the essence of the Christian faith was not dogmatic, ecclesial, juridical, and cultic, but rather the personal piety of individuals. Thus to Arnold, the so-called heretics in the history of the church often handed on the faith of the church more authentically than the church's major theologians and institutions. For example, while both the Magdeburg Centuries and the *Annales* praised Athanasius (d. 373) as the great defender of Trinitarian doctrine, Arnold faulted Athanasius for his ruthless and vindictive church politics. What Athanasius thought about doctrine was less important, Arnold claimed, than the effect doctrine had on his life. From this point of view, those whom the church had persecuted as heretics were now seen as the true Christians who had faithfully followed Jesus in opposing the "Babel" of the established church and the world. The Pietist concern with individuals and their religious experience foreshadowed later interests in biographical and psychological studies of historical figures.

But Arnold also remained in debt to the Eusebian model. For Arnold the consummate epoch of church history was the first three centuries, a time of origins he saw filled with the spirit of freedom, living faith, and holy living. The corruption and decay of the responsible love of the early church, Arnold believed – in stark contrast to Eusebius – began under the emperor Constantine, whose legitimation of the church in the Roman Empire introduced it to the temptations of power and wealth. Here then is the oft-repeated claim that when the church became the established church of the Roman Empire it "fell" and initiated a long decline into the state church so sharply criticized by Søren Kierkegaard's nineteenth-century *Attack Upon "Christendom."*

The above brief sketch of historiography suggests that the periodization of history as ancient, medieval, and modern so ingrained in modern thought, is itself a construct. The effort in more recent studies to expand awareness of the history of Christianity beyond the history of doctrines, the ideas of the elite, and the institutions that shape and convey these ideas reflects the awareness that there is more than one memory and identity of the Christian community in history. These more comprehensive efforts indicate that much historical writing has lacked attention to the roles of the poor, the oppressed, and women in the church, as well as the explosive growth of Christianity in Asia, Africa, and Latin America. The newer histories may thus serve the present by not only recalling hitherto unnoticed aspects of the past, but also by strengthening people's awareness of their own cause by giving voice to the voiceless, that they may engage in the conversations forming personal and communal identities.

Glossary

adiaphora "Matters of indifference" in faith and practice because they are neither banned nor mandated by scripture. Adiaphorist controversies erupted in the Reformation over the doctrinal implications of liturgical ceremonies and vestments when mandated by the government. The issue was whether such elements (e.g., sign of the cross, limitation of ordination to bishops, baptism with exorcism, images, etc.) compromised an evangelical understanding of justification and Christian freedom.

Anabaptism Literally, "re-baptism," a pejorative designation of those in the Reformation period who rejected infant baptism in favor of a "believer's baptism." Because the first generation had been baptized as infants, they were "re-baptized" upon their adult confession of faith. Members of the Anabaptist communities promoted a "free church" principle of a voluntary church.

Apocalypticism Eschatological expectations of the end of history associated with the books of Daniel and Revelation that forecast great upheavals, the appearance of the Antichrist, and the Last Judgment. Apocalyptic prophecies intend to warn the evil of their coming cataclysmic judgment and to console the righteous with the promise of God's deliverance (cf. Mark 13:14–27).

Apocrypha Those books in the Septuagint and Vulgate Bibles excluded by Protestants as non-canonical; also known as the Deuterocanonical books.

apologetic theology Expositions that defend the faith, especially through its interpretation in relation to reigning cultural challenges (e.g., second-century Greco-Roman and nineteenth-century European philosophies).

Arianism Belief that Christ is a creation of the Father, having an origin and consequently neither eternal nor equal to the Father, who received the title Son of God due to his foreseen righteousness. A favorite biblical text of Arians was Proverbs 8:22ff.: "The Lord created me at the beginning of his work, the first of his acts of long ago. Ages ago I was set up, at the first, before the beginning of the earth." Arianism was condemned by the councils of Nicaea (325) and Constantinople (381).

benefice An endowed church office.

bull From Latin *bulla*, "seal"; a written papal mandate attested by the pope's seal.

canon law Legislation that governs the faith, morals, and organization of the Roman Catholic Church.

celibacy Unmarried state required of Western clergy and religious since the twelfth century; rejected by the Protestant Reformers. The Eastern Orthodox Church permits marriage of priests and deacons before ordination but not after; bishops must be celibate.

chiliasm Also, millennialism; a historical variation on the theme of a future thousand-year reign of Christ's saints based on readings of Revelation 20.

communicatio idiomatum The communication or exchange of attributes. Advanced by Cyril of Alexandria, among others, during the Christological controversies; posits that although the human and divine natures of Christ are distinct, the attributes of one may be predicated of the other due to their union in the one person of Christ.

conciliarism The vesting of church authority in a general or ecumenical council; promoted at the councils of Constance (1414–18) and Basel (1431–49); sought reform of church and papacy through church councils.

confession (1) Private or public acknowledgment of sin. (2) Public profession of the principles of faith subscribed to by its adherents (e.g., the Augsburg Confession of 1530).

council A formal church assembly convened to regulate matters of faith and discipline. A provincial council is a meeting of bishops with their archbishop; a diocesan synod is a meeting of a bishop with the clergy of his diocese; an ecumenical or general council is a meeting of all bishops of the church under the leadership of the pope or the emperor.

cuius regio, eius religio "Whose [the prince's] rule, his religion"; the formula later used to describe the Religious Peace of Augsburg (1555) by which rulers were permitted to decide whether their land would be Roman Catholic or Lutheran.

decretals Papal letters of advice with the force of law; also, collections of papal responses to questions.

docetism A heretical Christology related to Gnosticism that claimed Christ's body only appeared to be real, and that therefore at the crucifixion Christ only seemed to suffer and die. Docetism reflects Gnosticism's distrust of the material world.

Donatism A fourth-century schismatic renewal movement in northern Africa that stressed that the validity of Word and sacraments was contingent upon the moral purity of the priest. In general, the view that the message is dependent upon the messenger.

Ebionitism Early Jewish-Christian ascetic sect whose name derives from Hebrew for "poor men." Their teachings are obscure, but the name is associated with a reductionist Christology positing Jesus was the son of Joseph and Mary upon whom a heavenly archangel descended at his baptism. Basically held that Jesus was a true prophet, but the law of Moses remains the way to salvation, not Jesus himself.

ecumenical movement From Greek *oikumene*, "the whole inhabited world"; the efforts begun in the twentieth century among Christian churches seeking unity of ministry and worship; the main models for which, "conciliar fellowship" and "reconciled diversity," developed, respectively, from the World Council of Churches and the Christian World Communions.

encyclical A circular letter addressed to churches, initially by any bishop but now restricted to papal letters.

eschatology Doctrine of the "last things": death, resurrection, Last Judgment, end of the world, eternal life.

Eucharist From Greek *eucharistein*, "to give thanks;" the name for the central act of worship. Also termed communion, Lord's Supper, and mass.

evangelical From Greek *euangelion*, literally "good news" (i.e., the gospel). Historically, the term was used by Reformers as a self-designation in opposition to the papal church; modern usage often denotes those conservative Protestant groups that stress an experienced conversion and the centrality of a fundamentalist interpretation of scripture.

ex opere operantis The efficacy of the sacraments related to the receiver's subjective disposition.

ex opere operato Sacramental validity is due to the performance of the rite; posits the objective validity of the sacraments apart from the subjective attitude of the priest or recipient.

exegesis The methodology of the interpretation of texts. The specific principles used in the exegesis of scripture are often referred to as hermeneutics.

filioque Latin: "and the Son." The clause added to the Nicene creed in the West that states that the Holy Spirit proceeds from the Father and the Son.

fundamentalism Definition of the Christian faith by a list of specific necessary or fundamental doctrines; especially associated with claim for the inerrancy or infallibility of scripture promoted by conservative elements within many denominations from the last part of the nineteenth century in reaction to the biblical criticism and the theory of evolution. The term itself derives from a series of 12 tracts entitled *The Fundamentals* (ca. 1909).

glossalalia From Greek, *glossa*, "tongue" or "language"; speaking or praying in unknown tongues; a practice of Pentecostal churches and charismatic communities.

Gnosticism Greek *gnosis*, "secret knowledge" as the way of salvation; term applied to a variety of early Christian groups that held to a dualistic view of the cosmos that opposed the spiritual world and material world, matter being evil; since the creation is associated with evil, Gnostics rejected the God of Creation, and the Hebrew scriptures, and posited a Christology that denied the real humanity of Christ (docetism). The creeds respond specifically to Gnostic claims in their first article that professes God is the creator of heaven and earth (i.e., the material world) and in their second article that Jesus was born, died, and was buried (in opposition to the docetic claim that the Christ only appeared to be human).

Humanism Intellectual–cultural movement of the European Renaissance focused on classical culture as the resource for the renewal or "rebirth" of Western culture and Christianity.

Jansenism A French Catholic movement associated with Cornelius Jansen's revival of Augustinian theology and the convent of Port-Royal. Theologically, Jansenism claimed good works are impossible without special grace from God, and that grace is irresistible (a kind of determinism). Jansenist antagonism to the Jesuits was famously expressed in Pascal's *Provincial Letters*. The movement was condemned as heretical by the Sorbonne (1649) and pope Innocent X (1653).

liberal theology/liberalism An imprecise term for theological currents beginning with Schleiermacher which attempted to incorporate modern critical analysis of orthodox faith by reason and experience; tendency of some Protestant groups influenced by the Enlightenment; optimistic view of the human condition that affirms human freedom in faith and ethics to respond to God's will (e.g., Pelagianism). In Roman Catholic theology liberalism is usually termed modernism.

modernism Roman Catholic version of Protestant liberalism that was open to the application of modern science and philosophy to theology. Condemned by pope Pius X in 1907.

monophysitism View that there is one divine nature of the Christ; refused to accept Chalcedonian Christology because it was seen as Nestorian.

Nestorianism View that there were two subsistent beings in Christ united in one external undivided appearance. Condemned at the Council of Chalcedon (451).

Pelagianism Positive view of human capability to merit salvation through free will to choose and accomplish works pleasing to God; downplays divine grace.

pentecostalism Christian communities and churches marked by belief that the experience of the first Christians on the day of Pentecost (Acts 1–2) continues in the present, including the gifts of tongues (glossalalia), prophecy, healing, and exorcism. Rooted in the Holiness movement, the first "Spirit baptisms" began at Bethel College, Topeka Kansas, and spread to Houston, Texas, and then Los Angeles, where W. J. Seymour initiated the famous Azusa Street revival. Among the larger Pentecostal churches are the Assemblies of God, the Church of God in Christ, and the International Church of the Foursquare Gospel. Pentecostalism has spread widely in recent decades throughout Latin America.

Protestant Orthodoxy Characterization of the post-Reformation generation of Protestant efforts to define "correct doctrine" in conformity with their confessions and in opposition to alternative confessions; also referred to as Protestant Scholasticism because of the embrace of rational methodology, Aristotelian philosophy, and parallels to medieval efforts to develop theological systems.

soteriology Greek, *soteria*; theological treatment of salvation.

transubstantiation The doctrine that posits that the bread and wine in the Eucharist are transformed into the body and blood of Christ while retaining their outward appearance. Defined at the Fourth Lateran Council (1215).

Vulgate The Latin translation of the Bible, dependent to a great extent upon the work of Jerome (d. 420); criticized by Humanists and Reformers of the Reformation period for numerous inaccuracies.

Further Reading

General Reference

Barrett, David, ed., *World Christian Encyclopedia*, New York: Oxford University Press, 2000.

Bettenson, Henry and Chris Maunder, eds., *Documents of the Christian Church*, Oxford: Oxford University Press, 1999.

Bradley, James E. and Richard A. Muller, *Church History: An Introduction to Research, Reference Works, and Methods*, Grand Rapids, MI: Eerdmans, 1995.

Brauer, Jerald C., ed., *The Westminster Dictionary of Church History*, Philadelphia, PA: Westminster, 1971.

Brown, Raymond E., et al., eds., *The New Jerome Biblical Commentary*, Englewood Cliffs, NJ: Prentice-Hall, 1990.

Burgess, Stanley M. and Gary B. McGee, eds., *Dictionary of Pentecostal and Charismatic Movements*, Grand Rapids, MI: Zondervan, 1988.

Campbell, Ted A., *Christian Confessions: A Historical Introduction*, Louisville, KY: Westminster John Knox, 1996.

Chadwick, H. and G. R. Evans, *Atlas of the Christian Church*, London: Macmillan, 1987.

Cross, F. L. and E. A. Livingstone, eds., *The Oxford Dictionary of the Christian Church*, Oxford: Oxford University Press, 2002.

Dowley, Tim, ed., *The Baker Atlas of Christian History*, Grand Rapids, MI: Baker, 1997.

Fahlbusch, Erwin, et al., eds., *The Encyclopedia of Christianity*, 5 vols., Grand Rapids, MI: Eerdmans, 1999–.

Ferguson, Everett, ed., *Encylcopedia of Early Christianity*, 2nd edn., New York: Garland, 1997.

Fitzgerald, Allan D., gen. ed., *Augustine through the Ages: An Encyclopdia*, Grand Rapids, MI: Eerdmans, 1999.

Hillerbrand, Hans J., ed.-in-chief, *The Oxford Encyclopedia of the Reformation*, 4 vols., New York: Oxford University Press, 1996.

Hillerbrand, Hans J., ed., *The Encyclopedia of Protestantism*, 4 vols., New York: Routledge, 2004.

Langer, William L., ed., *The Encyclopedia of World History*, 6th edn., Boston, MA: Houghton Mifflin, 2001.

Leith, John, ed., *Creeds of the Churches*, 3rd edn., Atlanta, GA: John Knox, 1982.

Littell, Franklin H., *Historical Atlas of Christianity*, New York: Continuum, 2001.

Lohse, Bernhard, *A Short History of Christian Doctrine from the First Century to the Present*, Philadelphia, PA: Fortress, 1966.

Lossky, Nicholas, et al., eds., *Dictionary of the Ecumenical Movement*, Grand Rapids, MI: Eerdmans, 1991.

Metzger, Bruce and Michael D. Coogan, eds., *The Oxford Companion to the Bible*, New York: Oxford University Press, 1993.

Muller, Richard A., *Dictionary of Latin and Greek Theological Terms*, Grand Rapids, MI: Baker, 1985.

New Catholic Encyclopedia, 17 vols., New York: McGraw-Hill, 1967–79.

Noll, Mark, et al., eds., *Eerdmans Handbook to Christianity in America*, Grand Rapids, MI: Eerdmans, 1983.

Pelikan, Jaroslav, *The Christian Tradition: A History of the Development of Doctrine*, 5 vols., Chicago, IL: University of Chicago Press, 1971–89.

Sunquist, Scott W., ed., *A Dictionary of Asian Christianity*, Grand Rapids, MI: Eerdmans, 2001.

Walton, Robert C., *Chronological and Background Charts of Church History*, Grand Rapids, MI: Zondervan, 1986.

Comprehensive Histories of Christianity

Aland, Kurt, *A History of Christianity*, 2 vols., Philadelphia, PA: Fortress, 1985.

Duffy, Eamon, *Saints and Sinners: A History of the Popes*, New Haven, CT: Yale University Press, 1997.

González, Justo L., *The Story of Christianity*, 2 vols., San Francisco: Harper and Row, 1984–5.

Irvin, Dale T. and Scott W. Sunquist, *History of the World Christian Movement, I: Earliest Christianity to 1453*, New York: Orbis, 2001.

Jedin, Herbert and John Dolan, eds., *History of the Church*, 10 vols., New York: Crossroad, 1987.

Kee, Howard C., et al., *Christianity: A Social and Cultural History*, 2nd edn., Upper Saddle River, NJ: Prentice-Hall, 1998.

MacHaffie, Barbara J., *Her Story: Women in Christian Tradition*, Philadelphia, PA: Fortress, 1986.

McManners, John, ed., *The Oxford History of Christianity*, Oxford: Oxford University Press, 1993.

Miles, Margaret R., *The Word Made Flesh: A History of Christian Thought*, Oxford: Blackwell, 2005.

Noll, Mark, *Turning Points: Decisive Moments in the History of Christianity*, 2nd edn., Grand Rapids, MI: Baker, 2003.

Historiography

Cantor, Norman F., *Inventing the Middle Ages*, New York: Quill, 1991.

Chesnut, Glenn F., *The First Christian Histories: Eusebius, Socrates, Sozomen, Theodoret, and Evagrius*, 2nd revd. edn., Macon, GA: Mercer University Press, 1986.

Gay, Peter, Victor G. Wexler, and Gerald Cavenaugh, eds., *Historians at Work*, 4 vols., New York: Harper and Row, 1972–5.

Harvey, Van A., *The Historian and the Believer: The Morality of Historical Knowledge and Christian Belief*, New York: Macmillan, 1966.

Niebuhr, Reinhold, *Faith and History: A Comparison of Christian and Modern Views of History*, New York: Scribners, 1949.

Wengert, Timothy J. and Charles Brockwell, Jr., eds., *Telling the Churches' Stories: Ecumenical Perspectives on Writing Christian History*, Grand Rapids, MI: Eerdmans, 1995.

Wilken, Robert L., *The Myth of Christian Beginnings: History's Impact on Belief*, Garden City, NY: Anchor Books, 1972.

Early Christianity

Brown, Peter, *Augustine of Hippo: A Biography*, Berkeley: University of California Press, 1967.

Brown, Peter, *The Cult of the Saints: Its Rise and Function in Latin Christianity*, Chicago, IL: University of Chicago Press, 1981.

Brown, Peter, *The Body and Society: Men, Women, and Sexual Renunciation in Early Christianity*, New York: Columbia University Press, 1988.

Brown, Peter, *The Rise of Western Christendom: Triumph and Diversity AD 200–1000*, Oxford: Blackwell, 1996.

Burton-Christie, Douglas, *The Word in the Desert: Scripture and the Quest for Holiness in Early Christian Monasticism*, New York: Oxford University Press, 1993.

Davis, Leo Donald, *The First Seven Ecumenical Councils (325–787): Their History and Theology*, Collegeville, MN: Liturgical Press, 1990.

Edwards, Mark, ed. and trans., *Constantine and Christendom: The Oration to the Saints, The Greek and Latin Accounts of the Discovery of the Cross, The Edict of Constantine to Pope Silvester*, Liverpool: Liverpool University Press, 2003.

Ehrman, Bart D., *Lost Christianities: The Battles for Scripture and the Faiths We Never Knew*, New York: Oxford University Press, 2003.

Ehrman, Bart D., *Lost Scriptures: Books That Did Not Make It into the New Testament*, New York: Oxford University Press, 2003.

Eusebius, *The History of the Church from Christ to Constantine*, trans. by G. A. Williamson, London: Penguin Books, 1965, rep. 1981.

Evans, Craig A. and Donald A. Hagner, eds., *Anti-Semitism and Early Christianity: Issues of Polemic and Faith*, Minneapolis, MN: Fortress, 1993.

Evans, G. R., *A Brief History of Heresy*, Oxford: Blackwell, 2003.

Evans, G. R., ed., *The First Christian Theologians: An Introduction to Theology in the Early Church*, Oxford: Blackwell, 2004.

Frend, W. H. C., *The Rise of Christianity*, Philadelphia, PA: Fortress, 1984.

Gregg, R. and D. Groh, *Early Arianism: A View of Salvation*, Philadelphia, PA: Fortress, 1981.

Hall, Stuart G., *Doctrine and Practice in the Early Church*, Grand Rapids, MI: Eerdmans, 1991.

Herrin, Judith, *The Formation of Christendom*, Princeton, NJ: Princeton University Press, 1987.

Hofstadter, Richard, *The Progressive Historians*, New York, 1968.

Hultgren, Arland J., *The Rise of Normative Christianity*, Minneapolis, MN: Fortress, 1994.

Hultgren, Arland J. and Steven Haggmark, eds., *The Earliest Christian Heretics: Readings from Their Opponents*, Minneapolis, MN: Fortress, 1996.

Kraemer, Ross and Mary Rose d'Angelo, eds., *Women and Christian Origins*, New York: Oxford University Press, 1999.

Rusch, William, ed., *The Trinitarian Controversy*, Philadelphia, PA: Fortress, 1980.

Wilken, Robert L., *The Christians as the Romans Saw Them*, New Haven, CT: Yale University Press, 1984.

Wilken, Robert L., *Remembering the Christian Past*, Grand Rapids, MI: Eerdmans, 1995.

Wilken, Robert L., *The Spirit of Early Christian Thought: Seeking the Face of God*, New Haven, CT: Yale University Press, 2003.

Medieval Christianity

Atkinson, Clarissa, *The Oldest Vocation: Christian Motherhood in the Middle Ages*, Ithaca, NY: Cornell University Press, 1991.

Bynum, Caroline Walker, *Holy Feast and Holy Fast: The Religious Significance of Food to Medieval Women*, Berkeley: University of California Press, 1987.

Duby, Georges, *The Three Orders: Feudal Society Imagined*, trans. by Arthur Goldhammer, Chicago, IL: University of Chicago Press, 1980.

Evans, G. R., ed., *The Medieval Theologians: An Introduction to Theology in the Medieval Period*, Oxford: Blackwell, 2001.

Gurevich, Aaron, *The Origins of European Individualism*, Oxford: Blackwell, 1995.

Hinson, E. Glenn, *The Church Triumphant: A History of Christianity up to 1300*, Macon, GA: Mercer University Press, 1995.

Hodges, R. and D. Whitehouse, *Mohammed, Charlemagne and the Origins of Europe*, Ithaca, NY: Cornell University Press, 1983.

Hussey, J. M., *The Orthodox Church in the Byzantine Empire*, Oxford: Clarendon, 1986.

Leclercq, Jean, et al., *The Spirituality of the Middle Ages*, London: Burns and Oates, 1968.

Leclercq, Jean, *The Love of Learning and the Desire for God*, London: SPCK, 1978.

Le Goff, Jacques, *The Birth of Purgatory*, London: Scolar Press, 1984.

Le Goff, Jacques, *Intellectuals in the Middle Ages*, Oxford: Blackwell, 1993.

Little, Lester K., *Religious Poverty and the Profit Economy in Medieval Europe*, Ithaca, NY: Cornell University Press, 1978.

Little, Lester K. and Barbara H. Rosenwein, eds., *Debating the Middle Ages: Issues and Readings*, Oxford: Blackwell, 1998.

Lynch, Joseph H., *The Medieval Church: A Brief History*, London: Longman, 1992.

Moore, R. I., *The Formation of a Persecuting Society: Power and Deviance in Western Europe, 950–1250*, Oxford: Blackwell, 1987.

Radice, Betty, trans., *The Letters of Abelard and Heloise*, London: Penguin Books, 1974.

Riley-Smith, Jonathan, ed., *The Oxford History of the Crusades*, Oxford: Oxford University Press, 1999.

Shahar, Shulamith, *The Fourth Estate: A History of Women in the Middle Ages*, London: Routledge, 1991.

Southern, R. W., *Western Society and the Church in the Middle Ages*, London: Penguin Books, 1970.

Sumption, Jonathan, *Pilgrimage: An Image of Medieval Religion*, London: Faber and Faber, 1975.

Tierney, Brian, *The Crisis of State and Church, 1050–1300*, Englewood Cliffs, NJ: Prentice-Hall, 1964.

Ullmann, Walter, *A Short History of the Papacy in the Middle Ages*, London: Methuen, 1972.

Vauchez, André, *Sainthood in the Later Middle Ages*, New York: Cambridge University Press, 1997.

Reformation

Bossy, John, *Christianity in the West 1400–1700*, Oxford: Oxford University Press, 1985.

Brady, Thomas A., Jr., Heiko A. Oberman, and James D. Tracy, eds., *Handbook of European History 1400–1600. Late Middle Ages, Renaissance and Reformation*, 2 vols., Leiden: Brill, 1994.

Cameron, Euan, *The European Reformation*, Oxford: Clarendon, 1991.

Dickens, A. G. and John M. Tonkin with Kenneth Powell, *The Reformation in Historical Thought*, Cambridge, MA: Harvard University Press, 1985.

Dixon, C. Scott, ed., *The German Reformation: The Essential Readings*, Oxford: Blackwell, 1999.

Edwards, Mark U., Jr., *Printing, Propaganda, and Martin Luther*, Berkeley: University of California Press, 1994.

Gordon, Bruce, ed., *Protestant History and Identity in Sixteenth-Century Europe*, 2 vols., Aldershot: Scholar Press, 1996.

Greengrass, Mark, *The Longman Companion to the European Reformation c. 1500–1618*, London: Longman, 1998.

Gregory, Brad S., *Salvation at Stake: Christian Martyrdom in Early Modern Europe*, Cambridge, MA: Harvard University Press, 1999.

Hendrix, Scott, *Recultivating the Vineyard: The Reformation Agendas of Christianization*, Louisville, KY: Westminster John Knox Press, 2004.

Hsia, R. Po-chia, ed., *A Companion to the Reformation World*, Oxford: Blackwell, 2004.

Lindberg, Carter, *Beyond Charity: Reformation Initiatives for the Poor*, Minneapolis, MN: Fortress, 1993.

Lindberg, Carter, *The European Reformations*, Oxford: Blackwell, 1996.

Lindberg, Carter, ed., *The Reformation Theologians*, Oxford: Blackwell, 2001.

Muller, Richard A., *The Unaccommodated Calvin: Studies in the Foundation of a Theological Tradition*, New York: Oxford University Press, 2000.

Oberman, Heiko A., *Luther: Man between God and the Devil*, New Haven, CT: Yale University Press, 1990.

O'Malley, John W., *Trent and All That: Renaming Catholicism in the Early Modern Era*, Cambridge, MA: Harvard University Press, 2000.

Pettegree, Andrew, ed., *The Reformation World*, London: Routledge, 2000.

Pettegree, Andrew, *Europe in the Sixteenth Century*, Oxford: Blackwell, 2002.

Wiesner, Merry E., *Women and Gender in Early Modern Europe*, Cambridge: Cambridge University Press, 1993.

Wiesner-Hanks, Merry E., *Christianity and Sexuality in the Early Modern World: Regulating Desire, Reforming Practice*, London: Routledge, 2000.

Williams, George H., *The Radical Reformation*, 3rd edn. Kirksville, MO: Sixteenth Century Journal Publishers, 1992.

Modern

Ahlstrom, Sydney E., *A Religious History of the American People*, New Haven, CT: Yale University Press, 1972.

Barth, Karl, *Protestant Theology in the Nineteenth Century: Its Background and History*, Valley Forge, PA: Judson Press, 1973.

Bays, Daniel H., ed., *Christianity in China from the Eighteenth Century to the Present*, Stanford, CA: Stanford University Press, 1996.

Bediako, Kwame, *Christianity in Africa: The Renewal of a Non-Western Religion*, Maryknoll, NY: Orbis, 1995.

Berger, Peter L., *Questions of Faith: A Skeptical Affirmation of Christianity*, Oxford: Blackwell, 2004.

Bruce, Steve, *Fundamentalism*, Oxford: Blackwell, 2000.

Cameron, Euan, ed., *Early Modern Europe: An Oxford History*, Oxford: Oxford University Press, 1999.

Crowner, David and Gerald Christianson, eds., *The Spirituality of the German Awakening*, New York: Paulist, 2003.

Ford, David F., ed., *The Modern Theologians*, Oxford: Blackwell, 1997.

Hempton, David, *The Religion of the People: Methodism and Popular Religion c. 1750–1900*, London: Routledge, 1996.

Holifield, E. Brooks, *Theology in America: Christian Thought from the Age of the Puritans to the Civil War*, New Haven, CT: Yale University Press, 2003.

Holifield, E. Brooks, *A History of Pastoral Care in America: From Salvation to Self-Realization*, Nashville, TN: Abingdon, 1983.

Hollenweger, Walter, *Pentecostalism: Origins and Developments Worldwide*, Peabody, MA: Hendrickson Publishers, 1997.

Holtrop, Pieter and Huch McLeod, eds., *Missions and Missionaries*, Woodbridge: Boydall Press, 2000.

Jenkins, Philip, *The Next Christendom: The Coming of Global Christianity*, New York: Oxford University Press, 2002.

Lindberg, Carter, *The Third Reformation? Charismatic Movements and the Lutheran Tradition*, Macon, GA: Mercer University Press, 1983.

Lindberg, Carter, ed., *The Pietist Theologians*, Oxford: Blackwell, 2004.

McGrath, Alister, *The Future of Christianity*, Oxford: Blackwell, 2002.

McLeod, Hugh, *Religion and the People of Western Europe*, New York: Oxford University Press, 1981.

McLeod, Hugh, ed., *European Religion in the Age of the Great Cities 1830–1930*, London: Routledge, 1995.

McLeod, Hugh and Werner Ustof, eds., *The Decline of Christendom in Western Europe, 1750–2000*, Cambridge: Cambridge University Press, 2003.

Marsden, George, *Fundamentalism and American Culture: The Shaping of Twentieth Century Evangelicalism 1870–1925*, New York: Oxford University Press, 1980.

Martin, David, *Tongues of Fire: The Explosion of Protestantism in Latin America*, Oxford: Blackwell, 1990.

Noll, Mark, et al., eds., *Evangelicalism: Comparative Studies of Popular Protestantism in North America, the British Isles, and Beyond, 1700–1990*, New York: Oxford University Press, 1994.

Noll, Mark, *American Evangelical Christianity: An Introduction*, Oxford: Blackwell, 2001.

Noll, Mark, *America's God, from Jonathan Edwards to Abraham Lincoln*, New York: Oxford University Press, 2002.

Raboteau, Albert J., *A Fire in the Bones: Reflections on African-American Religious History*, Boston, MA: Beacon, 1995.

Robert, Dana, *American Women in Mission: A Social History of Their Thought and Practice*, Macon, GA: Mercer University Press, 1996.

Robert, Dana, ed., *Gospel Bearers, Gender Barriers: Missionary Women in the Twentieth Century*, Maryknoll, NY: Orbis, 2002.

Schleiermacher, Friedrich, *The Christian Faith*, 2 vols., New York: Harper Torchbooks, 1963.

Walls, Andrew F., *The Missionary Movement in Christian History: Studies in the Transmission of Faith*, Maryknoll, NY: Orbis, 1996.

Ward, W. R., *The Protestant Evangelical Awakening*, Cambridge: Cambridge University Press, 1992.

Ward, W. R., *Faith and Faction*, London: Epworth, 1993.

Williams, Peter W., ed., *Perspectives on American Religion and Culture*, Oxford: Blackwell, 1999.

Index

"Jesus," "God," and biblical names are not indexed